THE ULTIMATE
Sushi
COOKBOOK
FOR BEGINNERS

**A Simple & Easy Step-by-Step Guide to Prepare
Deliciously Healthy Sushi Roll, Sashimi,
Nigiri, Tuna, Teriyaki, Tempura
& More Recipes at Home**

LEI YANMEI

Disclaimer:

Thank you for choosing our cookbook. We want to assure you that we always strive to give our hardest effort in compiling & presenting the recipes within this book. Transparency is extremely important to us & we have made every attempt to be as much transparent as possible regarding the sources & testing of these recipes. Our team has put in a lot of time & effort to gather a wide range of recipes, collecting them from numerous online & offline sources. These recipes have then been carefully tested in our restaurant to ensure their authenticity, taste & quality. Apart from our team, authenticity of these recipes has also been confirmed by our customer's feedback. While we have taken great care to provide accurate & reliable recipes, we must emphasize that individual cooking results may vary. Factors such as personal cooking skills, ingredient quality, equipment variations & environmental conditions can influence the outcome of a recipe. As a part of our commitment to transparency, we highly recommend you to go through the last page of this cookbook. This section illustrates necessary clarifications, revisions, or additional information that may be relevant to the recipes presented. Please be assured that we have put our utmost dedication into creating a valuable resource for your culinary adventures. We appreciate your trust & hope that you find joy & success in exploring the recipes within our cookbook.

Item Weight: 7.7 ounces
Dimension: 8.5x11-inches
ASIN – eBook: B0BRNV3NVD
ISBN – Hardcover: 979-8373711593
ISBN – Paperback: 979-8372692107

Contents

Introduction

Sushi, a Japanese dish, consisting of small pieces of raw fish or seafood served on vinegared rice. It has a long history in Japan & is thought to have originated from a method of preserving the fish by fermenting it with rice. This process, known as nare sushi, was popular in Japan as early as the Yayoi period (c. 300 BCE–300 CE). The rice used in nare sushi was eventually discarded & the process of pickling the fish with vinegar was introduced in the Muromachi period (1336–1573) to improve the taste & preservation of the dish.

Over time, sushi evolved into various forms, including oshi-sushi & hako-sushi, which involved pressing the fish & rice into shape with wooden moulds. The nigiri sushi that is popular today, it consists of a small rice ball topped with a slice of raw fish, became popular in the Edo period (1603–1868) in the city of Edo (now Tokyo). The term "sushi" means "sour-tasting," & is derived from the verb sui, which means "to be sour."

Sushi has gained worldwide popularity & can be found in many countries outside of Japan. It is often served in restaurants, but can also be made at home using various ingredients, including different types of fish, vegetables & seasonings. Sushi is often enjoyed with soy sauce, wasabi & pickled ginger & can be served in a variety of styles, including rolls (maki-sushi), hand-formed balls (temaki) & pressed squares (chirashi sushi). There are numerous types of sushi, including nigiri sushi, which consists of a small rice ball topped with a slice of fish or other topping & maki sushi, which is made by rolling up vinegared rice & fillings in seaweed. In Japan, sushi is often eaten at specialty sushi restaurants, where a skilled sushi chef, or itamae prepare it. These chefs undergo years of training to perfect their craft & they take great pride in the presentation & quality of their sushi.

When eating sushi in Japan, it is customary to follow certain manners, such as not mixing wasabi into the soy sauce, as the sushi chef has already seasoned the fish with the appropriate amount of wasabi. It is also considered impolite to rub your chopsticks together or to stick them upright in a bowl of rice, as these actions are associated with funeral rituals.

Overall, sushi is a delicious & healthy food that is enjoyed by people worldwide. If you have the opportunity to try it, be sure to appreciate the skill & artistry of the sushi chef & follow the proper manners to fully enjoy the experience.

The History of Sushi

The original form of sushi, known as nare-sushi, was a method of preserving fish by fermenting it in rice for several months. The fermented fish was then eaten with rice & this was the earliest form of sushi.

Over time, sushi evolved & developed into different forms, depending on the region & local specialties. Oshi-sushi & funa-sushi are two examples of these regional variations of sushi.

Haya-sushi, or "quick sushi," was a more recent innovation, developed in early 19th century by Hanaya Yohei. This form of sushi, which is now known as nigiri-sushi, consists of slices of raw fish served on top of small balls of vinegared rice. It became popular in Tokyo, particularly at sushi yatai (food stalls) & eventually spread throughout the rest of Japan.

It is interesting to note that the 1923 Kanto Earthquake may have played a role in the spread of sushi culture throughout Japan, as many Tokyo sushi chefs were forced to evacuate back to their hometowns & brought their skills & knowledge of sushi with them. This helped to introduce & popularize sushi in other parts of Japan.

Types of Sushi

There are many types of sushi, each with its own unique characteristics & ingredients. Here is a brief overview of the types of sushi you listed:

- Nigiri-sushi is the most common type of sushi & it consists of a slice of raw fish or other topping served on top of an oblong mound of vinegared rice. It is also known as Edo-mae sushi, as it originated in the Edo period in Tokyo.
- Gunkan-maki, or "battleship roll," is a type of sushi that is similar to nigiri-sushi, but it has a piece of seaweed wrapped around it to hold the topping in place. It is often used for toppings that are soft or loose, such as sea urchin or salmon roe.
- Maki-sushi is a sushi roll that is made by rolling up vinegared rice & fillings in seaweed. It is often eaten by hand & comes in many different sizes, such as futo-maki (thick-roll) & hoso maki (thin roll).
- Temaki-sushi is similar to maki-sushi, but it has a conical shape & is hand-eaten.
- Chirashi sushi, or "scattered sushi," is a type of sushi that consists of pieces of raw fish placed on top of a bowl of vinegared rice. It is a good option for those who want to try a variety of fish or a large quantity of one kind.
- Inari-sushi is a type of sushi that consists of vinegared rice stuffed inside a pouch of flavored fried tofu.
- Nare-sushi is a traditional form of fermented sushi that was the earliest form of sushi in Japan.

- Oshi-sushi, or "pressed sushi," is a type of sushi that is prepared by pressing cured fish & rice into a box or mold. It is popular in the Osaka & Kansai region of Japan.
- Sashimi is simply slices of raw fish, served without rice. It is mostly eaten as an appetizer or as part of a multi-course meal.

Nutrition of Sushi

It is true that sushi made with traditional ingredients like raw fish, rice & vegetables can be a healthy choice. However, as you mentioned, the nutritional value of sushi can vary depending on the ingredients used & how it is prepared.

For example, sushi rolls that contain mayonnaise or other high-fat ingredients can be higher in calories & fat than other types of sushi. Additionally, the sodium content of sushi can be high due to the use of soy sauce, which is often served as a condiment for dipping sushi.

It is also worth noting that sushi made with raw fish carries a risk of food poisoning, especially if the fish is not fresh or has not been properly handled & stored. To reduce this risk, it is important to choose sushi from reputable restaurants & ensure that the raw fish is handled & stored properly.

Overall, sushi can be a healthy choice as part of a balanced diet, but it is important to be mindful about the ingredients & preparation methods used & to consume it in moderation.

Ways of Serving

In traditional sushi restaurants in Japan, it is common for the sushi to be served on minimalist, Japanese-style plates that are made of wood or lacquer. These plates are often geometric in shape & may be monotone or have two colors. The choice of the plate is intended to complement the aesthetic qualities of the sushi & enhance the dining experience.

Many sushi restaurants offer set menus at a fixed price, where the chef selects a variety of dishes. These set menus are often graded in terms of price & quality, with the most expensive ones being the highest quality. In Japan, these set menus are often referred to as 松竹梅 (shō-chiku-bai), with "matsu" being the most expensive, "take" being in the middle & "ume" being the least expensive.

In addition to traditional sit-down sushi restaurants, there are also sushi restaurants that offer a more casual dining experience, often with an open dining room concept. These restaurants may have a conveyor belt, known as a "sushi train," that carries color-coded plates of sushi for customers to choose from. After finishing, the bill is calculated by counting the number of plates of each color that have been taken. Some newer sushi train restaurants use barcodes or RFID tags to track the elapsed time since the dish was prepared.

Sushi is typically served with soy sauce, wasabi & pickled ginger (shoga). These condiments are used to add flavor & enhance the taste of the sushi.

- Soy sauce is the most commonly used condiment for sushi & it is usually served in a small dish for dipping.
- Wasabi, also known as "Japanese horseradish," is a pungent green paste that adds a spicy kick to the sushi & has antibacterial properties.
- Pickled ginger (shoga), which is often pink or orange in color, is also used to cleanse the palate between bites of sushi & has antibacterial properties as well.

It is important to use these condiments sparingly, as they can overpower the delicate flavors of the sushi. It is also considered polite to dip the sushi in the soy sauce with the fish side down rather than pouring the soy sauce directly on top of the sushi. Overall, these condiments are an integral part of the sushi experience & are used to enhance the flavors & enjoyment of the dish.

Pantry Staples

1. Sushi Rice: Sushi rice is a type of Japanese short-grain rice that gets sticky when it's cooked & is used as the base for sushi bowls & rolls.
2. Nori Sheets: Nori Sheets are thin, dried sheets of seaweed that are used to cover sushi rolls.
3. Rice Vinegar: Fermented rice is used to make rice vinegar, which is used to season sushi rice & give it a sour taste.
4. Soy Sauce: Soy sauce is a salty, umami-rich sauce that can be used to season sushi or to dip it in.
5. Wasabi: Wasabi is a horseradish-based spicy green paste that is often served with sushi to make it hotter.
6. Pickled Ginger (Gari): It is thinly sliced ginger that has been pickled in sweet vinegar. It is served with sushi to make the taste buds feel better.
7. Sesame Oil: Sesame oil is added to some sushi recipes to make them taste better, especially when drizzled over rolls or mixed into sauces.
8. Rice Wine: A sweet Japanese rice wine called mirin is used in sauces for meat, fish & some kinds of sushi.
9. Sauces: Hot sauces like Sriracha & Spicy Mayo are used to spice up sushi rolls, especially ones with a spicy element.
10. Sesame Seeds: Sesame seeds are often used to decorate sushi rolls because they taste & feel nutty.
11. Fruits & vegetables: Cucumber, avocado, carrots & scallions are common sushi fillings that can be used raw or lightly cooked.
12. Fish & seafood: Tuna, salmon, shrimp, crab & eel are all popular choices & you can get them either raw (sashimi) or cooked.

13. Tobiko & Masago: Tobiko or Masago is the colorful roe of flying fish or smelt that is used to decorate or top sushi rolls.
14. Sushi Mat: A bamboo sushi mat is a mat made of bamboo that is used to roll sushi.
15. Wrapper: When making sushi rolls, plastic wrap or aluminum foil is used to cover the bamboo mat so that it doesn't stick.

Risk Involvements

There are several potential chemical & biological hazards associated with consuming sushi. One hazard is the presence of environmental contaminants, such as mercury, in certain types of fish that are used in sushi. Big marine predators, such as tuna, can accumulate top levels of mercury in their bodies, which can be harmful to humans when consumed in large quantities. Nursing mothers, pregnant women, & young kids are particularly vulnerable to the effects of mercury.

Another hazard is the risk of infection from pathogens that can be present in raw fish, such as sashimi. There are numerous types of parasites that can be found in raw fish, including Clonorchis Sinensis, Anisakis & Diphyllobothrium, which can cause various types of illness. In the European Union, regulations require that raw fish used in sushi be frozen at temperatures below -20°C (-4°F) for at least 24 hours in order to destroy any parasites.

Certain types of sushi, such as those made with fugu (pufferfish) & some types of shellfish, can also be toxic if not prepared carefully. Fugu, in particular, can contain a lethal dose of tetrodotoxin in its internal organs & must be cooked by a licensed chef who has passed a special test in Japan. Additionally, there have been instances where the species of fish being sold as sushi has been misidentified, leading to concerns about the accuracy of product labeling & the need for stricter regulation & analysis of seafood products.

The Recipes

Alaska Roll

Prep Time: 30 mins
Overall: 30 mins
Servings: 1 roll
Calories (Per Serving): 305

Ingredients:

1 nori sheet
½ cup prepared sushi rice
¼ avocado, sliced
2 oz smoked salmon
1 tbsp smoked salmon roe
Shredded daikon radish

Instructions:

1. Spread out the sushi rice evenly on a nori-sheet, leaving a 1-inch of border at top for air.

2. In a horizontal line across bottom half of the rice, spread the smoked salmon & sliced avocado.

3. Finally, put smoked salmon roe on top of the salmon. The fillings will stay inside if you roll the nori sheet tightly away from you.

4. Put the roll on a cutting board & use a clean sharp knife to cut it into six to eight pieces.

5. Sprinkle the shredded daikon radish on top of the sliced pieces. Soy sauce should be added right away. Enjoy!

Albacore Tuna Bowl

Prep Time: 5 mins
Cook Time: 10 mins
Overall: 15 mins
Servings: 2
Calories (Per Serving): 409

Ingredients

9 oz sashimi-grade albacore tuna

4 tbsp shredded nori seaweed (kizami nori)

1 tsp toasted white sesame seeds

1 green onion/scallion

3 shiso leaves (perilla/ooba)

½-inch ginger (½-inch, 1.3 cm)

½ tsp wasabi (optional)

2 servings of cooked Japanese short-grain rice (1 rice-cooker-cup about 180 ml) yields 2 servings (1.75 US cups)

- Sauce:

2 tbsp soy sauce

1 tbsp's sake

2 tbsp mirin

1 tbsp roasted sesame oil

Instructions

1. Gather together all of the ingredients.

2. In order to make the sauce, put up all of the ingredients for sauce in a small sauce-pan & bring them to a boil. Take the sauce off the heat & put it in a small bowl on ice on top of a bigger bowl.

3. Slice the scallions thinly, roll up the shiso leaves & then slice them thinly. Grate the ginger.

4. Cut the albacore tuna into slices about half an inch (1.3 cm) thick & let them sit in the sauce for 10-min.

5. To serve this delicious dish put steamed rice in the bowls & then sprinkle the shredded nori & sesame seeds on top & add thinly sliced albacore tuna. Add scallions, shiso leaves, ginger & wasabi to the dish as a garnish.

- For Storing:

1. You can put the leftovers in a container that won't let air in & keep them in the fridge for a day.

Ahi Sushi Cups

Prep Time: 40 mins
Cook Time: 30 mins
Extra Time: 45 mins
Overall: 1 hrs 55 mins
Servings: 6
Yields: 12 cups
Calories (Per Serving): 312

Ingredients

1 cup of sushi rice, rinsed
1 ¼ cups water
8 tsp rice vinegar, divided
1 tbsp white sugar
1 -oz ⅓ less fat cream cheese at room temperature
1 tbsp kosher salt, divided
cooking spray
2 tbsp lower-sodium soy sauce
1 tsp of dark sesame oil
¼ tsp crushed red pepper
1 pound sushi-grade ahi tuna, cubed
½ cup cucumber - peeled, seeded & diced
2 medium green onions, thinly sliced
1 large avocado, diced
½ tbsp black sesame seeds, lightly toasted

Instructions

1. Mix rice & water in a medium sauce-pan on medium-high heat & bring to a boil. Turn the heat down to low, cover & cook for about 20-min, or until the liquid is gone (do not uncover while cooking.) Take off the pan from the heat & let it sit for 10-min with the lid on.

2. While the rice is sitting, put 2 tbsp of vinegar & 2 tbsp of sugar in a relatively small microwave-safe bowl. Microwave on high for 30 to 45-sec, or until the mixture boils. Mix ingredients with a whisk until the sugar is gone. Mix the cream cheese & ½ tsp of salt together in a bowl with a whisk. With a rubber spatula, gently fold the vinegar mixture into rice & then let it sit for 5-min.

3. Coat 12 muffin cups with a lot of cooking spray. Lightly spray each of the 12 pieces of parchment paper that are 5-inches square with cooking spray. Press the squares of paper into muffin cups to make liners. Press about 2 ½ tbsp of rice into the bottom & up the sides of each muffin cup, using wet hands. Refrigerate for 30 to 40-min.

4. In a bowl, whisk together the last 2 tsp of vinegar, the last ½ tsp of salt, the soy sauce, the sesame oil & the red pepper. Tuna, cucumber, green onion & avocado should be added to the bowl. Toss them together gently.

5. Divide the tuna mixture evenly between the rice cups & sprinkle sesame seeds on top. Lift the edges of the parchment paper to lift the cups out of the pan gently.

Buffalo Chicken Sushi Roll

Prep Time: 22 mins
Overall: 22 mins
Servings: 4
Yields: 4 rolls
Calories (Per Serving): 522

Ingredients

¼ cup of French-fried onions (such as French's*)
¼ cup of hot pepper sauce
¼ cup of spicy mayonnaise
½ lb. of fully cooked breaded chicken breast tenderloins
1 carrot, peeled & cut into 4-inch matchsticks
1 celery stalk, cut into 4-inch matchsticks
4 cups cooked sushi rice
4 sheets nori (dry seaweed)

Instructions

1. In a bowl, combine the chicken & hot sauce & toss to coat.

2. Put one sheet of nori on a bamboo sushi mat. Spread about one cup of rice on the nori, leaving a ½-inch strip along one edge. Set ¼ of chicken, carrot & celery in a line near one edge of the rice. Carefully lift up the edge near the filling with the mat & roll the wrap tightly around the filling. Wet the last edge of the nori with water on your finger & press to seal. Repeat with the rest of the ingredients.

3. Use a sharp, wet knife to cut each roll into eight pieces. Add a small amount of French-fried onion & a dollop of mayonnaise to each piece.

California Roll Sushi

Prep Time: 40 mins
Cook Time: 20 mins
Extra Time: 30 mins
Overall: 1 hrs 30 mins
Servings: 8
Yields: 8 rolls
Calories (Per Serving): 232

Ingredients

¼ cup of mayonnaise
¼ cup of the rice vinegar
½ cup imitation crabmeat, finely chopped
1 cucumber, cut into thin spears
1 cup uncooked short-grain white rice
1 cup of the water
1 tbsp white sugar
2 ½ tbsp sesame seeds
2 avocados – must be pitted, peeled & sliced the long way
8 sheets nori (dry seaweed)

Instructions

1. Wash up the rice in several water changes until the rinse water is clear. Drain well & put the rice & 1 cup of water in a covered pan or rice cooker. Bring it to boil, then turn down heat down to low & cover the pan. Let the rice cook on low heat for about 15-min, or until the top looks dry. Turn off the heat & then let the rice sit for 10-min so that it can soak up the rest of water.

2. Mix rice vinegar & sugar in a tiny bowl until the sugar is dissolved, then stir \ mixture into cooked rice until it is well mixed. Let the rice cool down, then set it aside.

3. Mix the fake crab with the mayonnaise & set it aside. To roll the sushi, put plastic wrap over a bamboo rolling mat. Put a sheet of nori on the plastic wrap with the shiny side down. Using wet fingers, put a thin, even layer of cooked rice on the nori. Leave ¼-inch of the bottom edge of the sheet uncovered. About ½ tsp of sesame seeds is sprinkled on the rice & then the seeds should be gently pressed into the rice. Flip the nori sheet carefully so that the side with the seaweed is facing up.

4. Place two or three long spears of cucumber, two or three slices of avocado & about one tbsp of the crab mixture in a line across nori sheet, about ¼ of an inch from the edge that isn't covered. Take edge of the bamboo rolling sheet. Now fold the bottom edge up to cover the filling & tightly roll the sushi into a cylinder about 1 ½-inches in diameter. Once the sushi is rolled, place it on the mat & squeeze it gently to make it tight.

5. Use a very clean sharp knife dipped in water to cut each roll into 1-inch pieces.

California Roll Sushi Salad

Prep Time: 25 mins
Cook Time: 25 mins
Overall: 50 mins
Servings: 4
Yields: 4 servings
Calories (Per Serving): 490

Ingredients

⅛ cup's sake

¼ cup sugar

½ cup of rice wine vinegar

1 ½ cups sushi rice, or Japanese short-grain white rice

1 avocado, chopped

1 cup seeded & chopped cucumber

1 tbsp soy sauce, or to taste

12 -oz imitation crabmeat, flaked

2 cups water

Instructions

1. Run cold water through a strainer with the rice in it until the water runs clear. Add about 3 cups of water to a medium sauce-pan, add the rice & bring to a boil. Turn the heat down to low, cover & cook for about 20-min, or until the rice is soft & the water is gone.

2. In the meantime, mix rice wine vinegar, sugar & sake in a bowl that can go in the microwave. Microwave on high for about 1-min, or until all of the sugar is dissolved.

3. Cooked rice should be put in a large bowl. Add the vinegar mixture & stir until everything is well mixed. Let it sit for 2-min.

4. Stir again. Mix well after adding the fake crabmeat, cucumber & chopped avocado. Use soy sauce to add flavor to each dish.

Chaikin Sushi

Prep Time: 30 mins
Cook Time: 25 mins
Overall: 55 mins
Servings: 6
Yields: 6 pieces
Calories (Per Serving): 218

Ingredients

1 cup sushi rice, or Japanese short-grain white rice

3 eggs, beaten

¼ tsp salt

1 tbsp vegetable oil

3 tbsp rice vinegar

2 tbsp white sugar

1 tsp salt

2 tbsp black sesame seeds

6 sprigs of Italian parsley with long stems

Instructions

1. Bring some water to a boil in a pot. Stir the rice in. Turn down the heat, cover it & let it cook for 20-min. When the rice is done completely, put it in a big bowl & let it cool down until it is cool enough to handle.

2. In the meantime, beat the eggs with ¼ tsp of salt. Put some vegetable oil on the bottom of a pan & put it over medium heat. Once the pan is hot, add 1/6 of the egg mixture & spread it out evenly on the bottom. Cook the egg until it is almost set, then carefully flip it over & cook for a few-sec more to set the other side. Repeat with the rest of the egg to make a total of six thin sheets.

3. Mix vinegar, sugar & 1 tsp of salt in a small bowl. Microwave the mixture for a few-sec until it is hot, then stir until the sugar is dissolved. Mix sesame seeds & vinegar into warm rice.

4. To put the rolls together, put a big spoonful of rice in the middle of each egg sheet. Fold the paper into a square & tie it shut with a sprig of Italian parsley.

Chef John's Sushi Rice

Prep Time: 10 mins
Cook Time: 20 mins
Extra Time: 15 mins
Overall: 45 mins
Servings: 6
Calories (Per Serving): 247

Ingredients

2 cups of uncooked sushi rice
2¼ cups water
¼ cup seasoned rice vinegar, or more to taste

Instructions

1. Put the rice in a strainer & run cold water over it until the water runs clear, which should take about 2-min. Put a strainer over a bowl & let drain for about an-hour, or until almost dry. Move to a pot with a heavy bottom & a tight-fitting lid.

2. Add the water to rice. Set pot over medium to high heat & then bring to a simmer without stirring. As soon as the bubbles start to form on the surface & the rice starts to simmer, turn down the heat & cover the pan. Just cook for 10-min. Take off the heat, lift the lid for one-sec & then put it back on immediately. Give it 10 more-min.

3. Move the rice to a sheet pan with a rim & spread it out with a fork, fanning it with a magazine or something similar to help it cool down. About half of the rice vinegar should be sprinkled on the rice as you gently mix it. Keep fanning until the rice is just a little bit warmer than room temperature. Spread the rest of the rice vinegar over the rice & use a fork to mix it all together. A small amount of rice should be easy to shape into an oblong base for sushi, but it should fall apart easily when cut with a fork.

- Notes

I buy seasoned rice vinegar, but you can make on your own by mixing a cup of rice vinegar or cider vinegar, ½ cup of white sugar & 4 tsp of kosher salt.

You can also finish the rice in a big bowl by stirring & tossing it with a bamboo rice paddle. Rice that is tossed on a sheet pan may be a bit stickier.

Chirashi Cake & Temari Sushi

Prep Time: 40 mins
Overall: 40 mins
Servings: 1
Calories (Per Serving): 1053

Ingredients

1 Japanese or Persian cucumber (cut in half, thinly sliced)
1 package chirashi sushi mix (I used "Sushi Taro brand")
4 servings cooked Japanese short-grain rice (2 rice-cooker-cups (180 ml x 2 = 360 ml) yields-roughly 4 servings (3 ½ US cups)
kinshi tamago ((shredded) thin egg crepe)
Sakura denbu (seasoned codfish flakes)
- For Sushi Cake Decoration

10-12 pieces of sashimi-grade salmon
12 shrimp (boiled)
⅓-½ cup ikura (salmon roe)
2-3 snow peas (blanched, cut diagonally)

Instructions

- Chirashi Sushi

1. When the rice is done cooking, take some out & put it in a small bowl. Add Sakura Denbu to the bowl & stir to make pink rice.

2. Put the rest of the rice in a large bowl & while the rice is still hot, add one packet of Chirashi Sushi Mix. A rice paddle is used to fold everything together with the rice. Cut through the rice with a knife to separate the grains. Cover with a wet towel to keep it from drying out.

3. Make thin crepes with eggs. Save 1 egg crepe to make 2 Temari Sushi & cut the rest of the egg crepes into thin julienne strips.

- Assembling the Chirashi Sushi Cake

1. Prepare a round, square, small, or large container. First, put the egg crepe garnish made of shreds on the bottom. Make sure there are no empty spaces. Then put a ½-inch (1.3 cm) layer of pink rice on top & finally, a piece of Chirashi Sushi.

Place the sliced cucumber around the bowl between the rice & the container. The cucumber will look nice around the edge when you turn the bowl upside down.

2. Put it on a plate & decorate it however you want. For sashimi rose, you put half of one piece of sashimi on top of the next & roll them up.

- Making of Temari Sushi

1. The thin egg crepe should be cut in half & put on a piece of plastic wrap. Chirashi sushi should be put on top of the egg crepe & tightly wrapped. Keep it wrapped up until it's time to eat.

2. When you're ready to eat, take the Temari Sushi out of its wrapping & put it on a plate. Add a snow pea, half of a sliced shrimp & ikura to the top to make it look nice.

- For Storing:

1. Rice gets hard when it's stored in the fridge, so it's best to cover it with plastic wrap & a thick kitchen towel. Sushi cake without sashimi-grade fish can be kept for a few-hours in a cool place without being refrigerated.

Cheese & Crab Sushi Rolls

Prep Time: 20 mins
Cook Time: 20 mins
Overall: 40 mins
Servings: 2
Yields: 2 sushi rolls
Calories (Per Serving): 444

Ingredients

1 cup uncooked white rice

2 cups water

2 tbsp rice vinegar

1 tsp salt

2 sheets nori seaweed sheets

¼ cucumber, peeled & sliced lengthwise

2 pieces imitation crab legs

½ (3 -oz) package of cream cheese, sliced

1 tsp minced fresh ginger root

Instructions

1. In a sauce-pan over high heat, bring the rice & water to a boil. Turn the heat down to medium-low, cover & simmer for 20 to 25-min, or until the rice is soft & the liquid is gone. Mix in salt & rice vinegar. Let it cool down all the way.

2. Set out the sheets of seaweed. Wet your hands & spread the cooled rice evenly on each sheet, leaving a ½-inch gap along one edge.

3. Put strips of cucumber, imitation crabmeat & cream cheese on top of the rice in a straight line along the side opposite the gap.

4. Roll sushi from the toppings to the end of the seaweed sheet that isn't covered. Cut each roll into 5/6 pieces with a sharp, wet knife. Serve with a side of minced ginger.

Creamy Sushi Bake

Make sure one of the things in the seasoned seaweed is sesame oil.

Prep Time: 15 mins
Cook Time: 15 mins
Extra Time: 5 mins
Overall: 35 mins
Servings: 24
Yields: 24 portions
Calories (Per Serving): 131

Ingredients

1 -oz dried shiitake mushrooms
cooking spray
4 cups cooked short-grain rice
6 tbsp aji nori Furikake (seasoned seaweed & sesame rice topping)
1 (8 -oz) package of imitation crabmeat, shredded
½ cup mayonnaise
½ cup sour cream
1 -oz tobiko (flying fish roe) (Optional)
1 kamaboko (Japanese fish cake), sliced into matchsticks
12 (2 -oz) packages of seasoned Korean seaweed

Instructions

1. Set a rack in the oven about 6-inches away from the heat source & turn on the broiler.

2. Soak shiitake mushrooms in hot water for 5 to 10-min, or until they are soft.

3. In the meantime, grease a 9x13-inch baking-pan or a glass baking dish with a little oil. Spread the rice out in the pan that has been prepared & then sprinkle the Furikake on top.

4. Drain the water from the mushrooms & squeeze them. Mix the mushrooms, crabmeat, mayonnaise, sour cream, tobiko & kamaboko. Put it on top of the Furikake.

5. Broil in a hot oven for about 15-min, or until the top is lightly browned. Cut the cake into 24 pieces & serve each one in the pan. Put a lot of the food on a seaweed sheet, wrap it loosely & eat it right away.

- Notes

Cucumber & Avocado Sushi

Prep Time: 35 mins
Cook Time: 25 mins
Extra Time: 5 mins
Yields: 24 rolls
Calories (Per Serving): 171

Ingredients

1 ¼ cups water
1 cup of uncooked glutinous white rice (sushi rice)
3 tbsp rice vinegar; 1 pinch salt
4 sheets nori (dry seaweed)
½ medium cucumber, sliced into thin strips
1 medium avocado - peeled, pitted & sliced

Instructions

1. Water & rice should be put in a pot & brought to a boil. Cover, turn the heat down to low & simmer for about 20-min, or until the rice is soft & the water is gone. Take off the pan from the heat, add the vinegar & salt & set it aside for at least 5-min to cool.

2. Wrap plastic wrap around a bamboo sushi mat to keep rice from sticking to it. Put one sheet of nori on top of the plastic. Spread the rice out evenly on a sheet of nori, leaving about ½-inch at the bottom open.

3. Put the avocado & cucumber in the middle of the rice. Pick up the mat, roll it once over the vegetables & then press down. Unroll the nori, then roll it again toward the end that isn't covered. This will make a long roll. If needed, add a little water to the seal roll. Repeat until all the rolls are made. Cut each roll into six pieces with a sharp, wet knife.

Cucumber Wrapped Sushi

Prep Time: 45 mins
Overall: 45 mins
Servings: 15
Calories (Per Serving): 75

Ingredients

About 2 Japanese or Persian cucumbers (or 1 English cucumber)
3-4 cups sushi rice (cooked & seasoned)
- Toppings of your choice:
4 oz sashimi-grade salmon
4 oz sashimi-grade yellowtail
4 ozsalmon roe sashimi grade tuna
4 tbsp ikura (salmon roe)
10 sashimi-grade shrimp (amaebi)
- For Garnishing
10 shiso leaves (perilla/ooba)
1 green onion/scallion
1 lemon
1 bunch kaiware daikon radish sprouts

Instructions

1. Get all of the ingredients together. I also use a round cookie cutter that is 1 ¾-inches (4.5 cm) wide.
- To Prepare the Fillings
1. Cut the tuna into small pieces & then mix it with a little scallion, soy sauce & sesame oil.
2. Using a peeler, cut the cucumber into long, thin strips.
- To Assemble
1. Put shiso leaves on a platter to serve. Dip a cookie cutter in a bowl of water (so rice doesn't stick) & put it on top of a shiso leaf. Half-fill the cookie cutter with sushi rice & carefully takes it out. One strip of cucumber slice is used to measure the circle's circumference by rolling the sushi into a cylinder.
2. Use a knife to cut slits at the end of the cucumber slice, as shown below. Now you can make the strip fit around the rice by weaving it.

3. Put your favorite toppings inside the cucumber-wrapped sushi. For amaebi, which is sweet shrimp, I put a few pieces from the outside to the middle of the cucumber cup, making it look like a flower.
4. Cut the sashimi-grade fish across the muscle, which is the white line in the fish & put a few slices in the cucumber cup.
5. Put the tuna mixture in the cup made from the cucumber. Add a slice of lemon & sprouts of kaiware daikon radish. Serve right away.
- For Storing:
1. I don't think you should keep fish & shrimp that are good for sashimi for more than 24-hours. Keep them cold until you're ready to serve them.

Dragon Roll

Prep Time: 30 mins
Cook Time: 5 mins
Overall: 35 mins
Servings: 1 roll
Calories (Per Serving): 515

Ingredients

1 sheet nori
½ cup prepared sushi rice
¼ ripe avocado, sliced
4 oz fresh eel, grilled
2 tbsp eel sauce
½ tsp sesame seeds

Instructions

1. Grill the fresh eel for 5 minutes on each side over high heat. Cut the eel into long strips.

2. Evenly spread the ready sushi rice on a nori sheet, leaving a 1-inch border around the top.

3. Lay the eel & avocado strips out flat on the bottom half of the rice.

4. Tightly roll the nori sheet away from you to seal the food inside.

5. Put the roll on a cutting board & use a sharp knife to cut it into 6 to 8 even pieces.

6. Spread eel sauce on top in a zigzag pattern. Add sesame seeds as a garnish & serve right away.

Futomaki Rolls

Prep Time: 20 mins
Cook Time: 5 mins
Overall: 25 mins
Servings: 4 rolls
Calories (Per Serving): 300

Ingredients

4 sheets nori
2 cups sushi rice
1 avocado, sliced
1 carrot, julienned
4 oz imitation crab sticks, sliced
½ cucumber, sliced
2 tbsp sesame seeds
4 tbsp seasoned rice vinegar

Instructions

1. Put cooked sushi rice & seasoned rice vinegar in a bowl & mix them together.

2. Place the nori sheet on the bamboo rolling mat so that it is flat.

3. Spread ¼ of the nori sheet with ½ cup of sushi rice, making sure not to go up an inch above the top.

4. Put a quarter of the vegetables & crab sticks across the middle of the rice in a horizontal line.

5. Lift the bottom edge of the nori with the mat & roll it tightly forward over the filling. Things should be tucked under the seam as you roll forward to make a tight roll.

6. Take the mat off. A sharp knife can be used to cut the roll into 6 to 8 pieces. Do it again with the rest of the ingredients.

7. Top with sesame seeds & serve with soy sauce for dipping. Enjoy!

Garlic Soy Marinated Albacore

Prep Time: 5 mins
Cook Time: 5 mins
Overall: 10 mins
Servings: 2
Calories (Per Serving): 176

Ingredients

7 oz sashimi-grade albacore tuna
2 cloves garlic
1 scallion
1 knob ginger (1-inch, 2.5 cm)
1 tbsp roasted sesame oil
4 tbsp soy sauce
- Optional Garnish

1 tbsp yuzu-flavored tobiko (flying fish roe)

Instructions

1. Gather all the ingredients together.

2. Garlic & scallions need to be cut up. Shred the ginger.

3. In a small pan, heat the sesame oil with medium heat. When the oil is too hot, add the garlic slices.

4. Cook the garlic until it smells good, then stir in the soy sauce.

5. Bring the sauce to boil & then turn down the heat & let it cook for 15 to 20-sec. Take off the heat.

6. Cut the albacore tuna into slices that are about 14-inch thick (6 mm). Put the tuna on a plate & brush it with the garlic sauce. Add scallion & ginger to the top & then sprinkle with tobiko. Serve right away.

Garlic Teriyaki Edamame

Prep Time: 10 mins
Cook Time: 10 mins
Overall: 20 mins
Servings: 4
Yields: 4 servings
Calories (Per Serving): 261

Ingredients

¼ cup water
3 cloves garlic, minced
1 (16 -oz) package of frozen edamame in the pod
¼ cup teriyaki sauce
2 tbsp brown sugar
2 tbsp rice vinegar
1 tbsp sesame oil
2 tbsp sesame seeds

Instructions

1. Over high heat, bring the water & garlic to a boil in a sauce-pan. Stir in the edamame & cook for about 5-min, or until the edamame is hot & most of the liquid has evaporated. Turn the heat down to medium-high & stir in the teriyaki sauce, brown sugar, vinegar & sesame oil. For about 4-min, stir the edamame while the sauce thickens & coats the beans. To serve, sprinkle sesame seeds on top.

Grilled Bacon Sushi Roll

Prep Time: 15 mins
Cook Time: 35 mins
Overall: 50 mins
Servings: 4
Yields: 1 roll
Calories (Per Serving): 660

Ingredients

6 thick slices of bacon
½ pound lean ground beef
1 tbsp barbeque spice rub, or to taste
4 thin slices prosciutto
2 jalapeno peppers sliced into long strips
2 sticks pepper Jack cheese
2 tbsp barbeque sauce, or to taste
1 cup French-fried onions

Instructions

1. Place bacon slices on a sushi mat so that the long sides are facing each other.

2. Mix together the ground beef & the spice rub. Spread in a thin layer over the bacon, leaving 1-inch of bacon uncovered at the end farthest from you. Prosciutto goes on top of the beef. Stack the strips of jalapeno on end closest to you. Next to the jalapeno strips, put the cheese sticks.

3. Tightly roll the bacon toward the end that is left open.

4. Heat the grill to 350°F (175°C). Cook the bacon roll seam side down over indirect heat for about 25-min, or until it is crisp. Put on some barbecue sauce.
Keep grilling for about 5-min, or until the barbecue sauce is glazed. Add the rest of the barbecue sauce & cook for another 5-min.

5. Take it off the grill & spread fried onions all over it. Cut it up & use chopsticks to eat it.

- Notes

Not interested in grilling it? Follow the same steps in an oven that has heated to 350°F (175°C).

Hosomaki Sushi Rolls

Prep Time: 1 hr
Overall: 1 hr
Servings: 10
Calories (Per Serving): 205

Ingredients

- For Sushi Rice

About 3 rice cooker cups of uncooked Japanese short-grain rice (3 rice cooker cups (180-ml x 3 = 540-ml) makes about five to six servings (5 ¼ US cups or 990 g). If you want to make sushi, you must use short-grain Japanese rice.

540 ml water.

1 piece of kombu (dried kelp; 5 grams; 2-inches x 2-inches or 5 cm by 5 cm; optional, but gives a nice smell!).

⅓ cup plain rice vinegar (you can use sushi vinegar, which is seasoned rice vinegar, instead).

3 tbsp sugar (you can skip if you are using bottled sushi vinegar).

1 ½ tsp of kosher salt (Diamond Crystal; use ½ for table salt) (you can skip if you are using bottled sushi vinegar).

- For Fillings

1 Japanese or Persian cucumber (yield 8 rolls)

7 oz sashimi-grade tuna (yield 12 rolls)

1 box natto (fermented soybean) (yield 2 rolls)

- For Tezu (Finger Dipping Water)

¼ cup water

2 tsp rice vinegar (unseasoned)

- Anything Else

5 sheets nori (dried laver seaweed)

soy sauce

wasabi (optional)

sushi ginger (gari)

Instructions

1. Gather up all the ingredients together. Please note that cook time doesn't include the time it takes to cook rice, which varies based on your device or method. A bamboo sushi mat is needed.

- To Make the Sushi Rice

1. This recipe calls for 3 rice cooker cups of uncooked rice, which will make 5 ¼ US cups & 10 Hosomaki (thin sushi rolls).

2. Use my recipe for sushi rice. Cover the sushi rice & rolls at all times with a damp cloth or with a plastic wrap, so they don't dry out.

- To Make the Fillings

1. Cut the cucumber off at both ends. Then cut it in half along its length & then in ½ again, so that you have 4 strips. Use a knife to remove the seeds, then cut the fruit in half lengthwise. You should have 8 strips of cucumber at the end.

2. Cut the tuna into thin slices (¼ to ½-inch) & then long strips (¼ to ½-inch) of the same thickness.

3. Take the natto out of the container & season it with soy sauce or the seasonings that came with the package. Mix it all together until it gets slimy & bubbly.

- To Roll the Sushi

1. In a small bowl, mix water & rice vinegar to make Tezu, which is finger-dipping water with vinegar. If you put this water on your hands, the rice won't stick to them.

2. Half the nori. Even though it looks like it, Nori sheets are not perfectly square. To make them square, cut the longer side in half. Also, nori goes bad quickly, so keep it in an airtight bag & only take out what you need.

3. Put the sushi mat on a surface you can work on. So, you can roll them up, the bamboo strings should go sideways & place the half sheet of nori on the bamboo mat- so that one of its long sides is near the back edge of the mat. Leave about three or four slats showing on the side that faces you. The shiny side of the nori should be on the bottom.

4. Before you touch the sushi rice, you should wet your hand.

5. Put ½ cup (90 g) of sushi rice into your hand using a ½-cup measuring cup. This way, each roll will have the same amount of rice & be the same size. Make sure to get the measuring cup, so the rice doesn't stick. I know this isn't the "right" way to do it, but until you can always get the right amount of rice, this will do!

6. Put the sushi rice in the middle of the nori on the left side. Now, spread the rice over the nori, leaving a 1-inch space along the top edge of the nori. Spread the rice to the right with your right hand & keep it away from the 1" space on top of the nori with your left fingers.

7. Spread the rice out evenly with both fingers, leaving a 1-inch space on top. If the rice starts to stick to your fingers, then dip them in the water.

8. Put the filling in the middle of the rice. This could be tuna, cucumber, or natto. If your tuna or cucumber is a little too short, add extra pieces to the end. Use your fingers to hold the filling down.

9. Roll the sushi over the filling & stop right where the edge of the rice is (you must still be able to see the 1" nori space after rolling).

10. Don't move the sushi mat yet. Use your fingers outside of the mat to gently shape & tighten the roll. Square off the sushi roll (or round). Then, lift the sushi mat & turn the roll one time to seal the nori. Again, gently squeeze the roll with your fingers to make it tighter.

11. Wet your knife with a damp towel & then cut the roll in half to cut it. When cutting through the sushi, you should "push & pull" the knife. Again, wet the knife & cut each half-roll into three pieces. Use soy sauce, wasabi & pickled ginger to go with the food.

- For Storing:
  1. While freshly made sushi rolls are best eaten immediately, they will be kept well in the fridge for up to 24-hours. I strongly suggest putting them inside an airtight container or a plate wrapped tightly in plastic.
  2. Then, wrap a thick kitchen towel around the container or plate, so the food stays safe in a cool place & the rice doesn't get hard from the cold air in the fridge.

Homemade Sushi

Prep Time: 40 mins
Cook Time: 25 mins
Overall: 1 hrs 5 mins
Servings: 8
Yields: 4 cut rolls
Calories (Per Serving): 152

Ingredients

1 ⅓ cups water

⅔ cup uncooked short-grain white rice

3 tbsp rice vinegar

3 tbsp white sugar

1 ½ tsp salt

4 sheets nori seaweed sheets

½ pound imitation crabmeat, flaked

1 avocado - peeled, pitted & sliced

½ cucumber, peeled, cut into small strips

2 tbsp pickled ginger

Instructions

1. Set the oven temperature to 300°F. (150°C).

2. In a medium pot, bring some water to boil & stir in rice. Turn the heat down to medium-low, cover & simmer for 20 to 25-min, or until the rice is soft & the water has been absorbed.

3. In a small bowl, combine rice vinegar, sugar & salt. Mix gently into the pot of cooked rice & set aside.

4. Put sheets of nori on a baking sheet.

5. Warm the nori for 1 to 2-min in an oven that has already been turned on.

6. Put 1 sheet of nori in the middle of a bamboo sushi mat. Spread out a thin layer of rice on top with wet hands. Set ¼ of the crabmeat, avocado, cucumber & pickled ginger in a line down the very center of the rice. To make a full roll, lift up one end of the mat & tightly roll it over the filling. Do this with the rest of the ingredients.

7. Cut each roll into 4 to 6 pieces with a wet, sharp knife.

- Tips

If you can't manage a bamboo sushi mat, a clean dish towel is the easiest way to roll sushi.

Inari Sushi

Prep Time: 30 mins
Servings: 3-4
Calories (Per Serving): 98

Ingredients

- For Sushi Rice

About 2 rice cooker cups uncooked Japanese short-grain rice (2x 180ml= 360 ml; 2 rice cooker cups yield about 3-4 servings (3 ½ US cups or 660g); makes about 12 Inari sushi pieces).
1 piece kombu (dried kelp) (5 g; 2-inches x 2-inches, 5cm x 5cm; optional, but it will give a nice aroma!).
2 tbsp sugar.
4 tbsp rice vinegar (unseasoned).
1½ cups of water (cook the rice on firm side as it needs to be seasoned with sushi vinegar; the rice to water ratio for sushi rice is 1-to-1, instead of 1 to 1.1 or 1.2 for normal steamed rice).
1 tsp of kosher salt (Diamond Crystal; use ½ for the table salt).

- For Inari Sushi

1 tbsp toasted white sesame seeds
12 Inari age (seasoned fried tofu pouch)

- For Garnish

sushi ginger (gari)
5 shiso leaves

Instructions

- To Make Sushi Rice

1. Gather up all the ingredients together. Make sushi rice in advance.

2. Use your fingers to gently wash the rice in a circular motion & rinse it a few times until the water is clear. Pour the water through a fine-mesh sieve & shake off any extra water.

3. Put the well-drained rice in the rice cooker bowl & fill the pot with water until it's just below the 3-cup line. If rice cooker has a "Sushi-Rice" setting, fill it with water until the line. Put the kombu on top of rice & let the rice soak in the water for 20–30-min & then start cooking. If you don't get a rice cooker, you can always cook the rice in a heavy-bottomed pot on stove or in an Instant Pot with the amount of water I wrote in this recipe.

4. Mix rice vinegar, sugar & salt in a small bowl to make sushi vinegar. Put it in the microwave for 30–40-sec, or until all of the sugar is dissolved. You can also use a sauce-pan to heat the sushi vinegar.

5. When the rice is done, you can throw away the kombu. If you're using a wooden sushi oke, also called a "hangiri," make sure to run water over it & let it drain well. Move the cooked rice to the sushi oke, a big bowl, or a baking sheet lined with parchment paper. Spread the rice out so it will cool more quickly.

6. Pour the sushi vinegar over the rice slowly while it is still hot. Keep it at a lukewarm/room temperature. Gently "cut" the rice at a 45-degree angle with a rice paddle to mix in the sushi vinegar mixture & separate the pieces of rice. Don't stir or mix the rice, or the grains might break & the rice will get mushy. Fan the rice hard with a paddle fan or different type of fan as you slice it in this way. This cools the rice & gets rid of any extra water. The rice gets shiny & doesn't get mushy when it's fanned. Cover the sushi rice you've made with a damp towel (or paper-towel) & leave it at the room temperature for a few-hours.

- To Make Inari Sushi

1. Let's make some Inari sushi now! Get the inari age out of the refrigerator.

2. Sprinkle sesame seeds on the sushi rice & use your fingers to "slice" the rice together. Cut the sushi rice into four parts (make 3-Inari sushi pieces with each quarter of sushi rice).

3. Drain the Inari age & save the juice or cooking liquid. Use it to wet your hands, then put a small handful (¼ cup) of sushi rice in your palm.

4. Make a long shape with the sushi rice. Do the same thing with the rest of the rice. There should be enough rice for 12 rice balls.

5. Carefully separate the skin all the way to the bottom of the Inari age pockets (be gentle as the skin is thin). On top, fold the skin outward.

6. Fill each Inari age with a rice ball. The sushi rice should go all the way to the corners, making them look smooth & round.

7. Fold both edges of the Inari age down to close it.

8. Then, fold the rest of the rice ball's edges in to seal it. Put the seam side down & keep making the rest of the Inari age. You can keep leftover Inari age in the freezer with the liquid for up to a month. If you put it in a container with a lid & put it in the fridge, you should use it within two to three days.

9. Kansai-Style: A different way to make Inari Sushi is to put colorful ingredients on top. Keep the top of the bag open & tuck the edges of the Inari age into the pocket so that the edges are smooth & round. The top can be decorated however you want. I used sliced cucumber, ikura (salmon roe), kinshi tamago (shredded egg crepe) & cooked salmon flakes in this dish.

- To Serve

1. Inari Sushi should be served at room temperature. If you want, you can decorate with shiso leaves & sushi ginger.

- For Storing:

1. Leftovers can be kept for a few-hours in a cool place, but they should be eaten on the same day they are made. They can be kept in fridge about 24-hours. I think the best way to store them is in a tight container with a tight lid or on a plate wrapped tightly in plastic & then wrapped in a thick kitchen towel. So, the food stays safe in a cool place, but the cold air in the fridge doesn't make the rice hard.

Inside-Out Spicy Tuna & Avocado Sushi

Prep Time: 30 mins
Cook Time: 30 mins
Overall: 1 hrs
Servings: 2
Yields: 6 rolls
Calories (Per Serving): 750

Ingredients

- Sushi Rice:

⅓ cup Japanese sushi-style rice
⅓ cup water
2 ¼ tsp rice vinegar
2 ¼ tsp white sugar
1 tsp salt

- Sushi Rolls:

4 -oz sashimi-grade yellowfin tuna, cut into small chunks
⅓ cup mayonnaise
3 tbsp chile oil, or more to taste
1 tbsp sesame oil
1 tbsp sriracha sauce
1 green onion, diced
3 sheets nori, cut in half
½ small ripe avocado, thinly sliced
¼ English cucumber, cut into matchsticks

Instructions

1. Use a strainer to rinse the rice until water runs clear.

2. Make the rice for sushi: In a sauce-pan, put the rice & water & bring to a boil. Turn the heat down to low, cover & cook for about 20-min, or until the rice is soft & the water is gone.

3. Mix rice vinegar, sugar & salt in a small sauce-pan over low heat. Stir for 1 to 2-min, or until the sugar is dissolved. Pour over the rice & mix until the rice has cooled & looks dry.

4. Make the rolls of sushi: With a fork, mash the tuna, mayonnaise, chile oil, sesame oil, Sriracha sauce & green onion in a bowl to break up some of the bigger pieces. Leave a few pieces whole to give the dish texture.

5. Wrap plastic wrap around a bamboo mat for rolling sushi. Place a sheet of nori with shiny side down on the mat. On top of the nori, spread a thin layer of rice. Spread slices of avocado over the rice. Turn the nori sheet over so the avocado is on the mat. Spread a thick layer of the tuna mixture about ¾ of the way down the back of the nori & then put matchsticks of cucumber on top.

6. Use the rolling mat to roll the sushi & use the plastic wrap to tuck in the ends. Take the sushi roll out of the plastic wrap & put it on a plate.

7. Do the same thing with the rest of the nori, rice, avocado, tuna mixture & cucumber.

- Notes

If you have certain medical conditions, eating raw seafood may make you more likely to get sick from food.

Instant Pot* Sushi Rice

Prep Time: 20 mins
Cook Time: 15 mins
Extra Time: 20 mins
Overall: 55 mins
Servings: 6
Yields: 3 cups
Calories (Per Serving): 146

Ingredients

1 cup Japanese sushi-style rice
1 (2-inch) piece kombu (Japanese dried kelp)
1 ¼ cups water
3 tbsp Japanese rice wine
1 tbsp hon-mirin (Japanese mirin)
¾ tbsp white sugar
½ tsp sea salt

Instructions

1. Put rice in the insert of a multi-function pressure cooker (like an Instant Pot*). Add enough water to cover the rice & rinse it while stirring in a circle. Use a sieve to separate things. Repeat about 5 times, or until the water comes out clear. Spread the rice out on a clean cloth for 10 to 15-min to dry.

2. Use a damp towel to gently clean the kombu, but don't take off the white powder. This is important for the umami flavor.

3. Break off a small piece of the kombu & put it in a small sauce-pan. Give the Instant Pot* to the rest of the kombu. Add 1 ¼ cups of water to the rice. Close the lid & lock it. Follow the instructions from the manufacturer & set the timer for 2-min. Give it 10 to 15-min to build up pressure.

4. Add rice wine, hon-mirin, sugar & sea salt to the pan. Heat on low until the sugar & salt are dissolved, but don't let it boil.

5. Using the manufacturer's instructions, let the pressure out using the natural-release method. This takes about 8-min. Using the quick-release method, carefully let out any extra pressure. Unlock the lid & take it off.

6. Using a rice paddle, carefully scrape the rice into a glass or ceramic bowl. Take out the kombu & throw it away. Take the smaller piece of kombo out of the vinegar mixture & throw it away. The rice paddle is used to cut the vinegar mixture into the rice. Stir in the vinegar mixture until the rice is smooth & there are no more lumps. Let the temperature drop to room temperature. You can fan the rice with a piece of cardboard to help it cool faster.

Korean Sushi (Kimbap)

Prep Time: 30 mins
Cook Time: 30 mins
Overall: 1 hrs
Servings: 6
Yields: 24 sushi pieces
Calories (Per Serving): 492

Ingredients

2 cups uncooked short-grain white rice
2 cups water
2 tbsp cider vinegar
2 leaves chard
2 eggs, well beaten
2 tbsp soy sauce, divided
3 tbsp water
1 onion, diced
1 tbsp vegetable oil
¾ pound beef tenderloin, minced
1 (5 -oz) can tuna, drained
1 carrot, julienned
1 cucumber, julienned
6 sheets nori (dry seaweed)

Instructions

1. Bring 2 cups of water & cider vinegar to a boil in a medium sauce-pan. Stir the rice in. Turn down the heat, cover & let the rice cook for 20-min, or until the grains are soft & sticky.

2. Put enough water in a medium sauce-pan to cover the chard. Bring to a boil & cook until the veggies are soft. Make narrow strips.

3. Whisk the soy sauce & 3 tbsp of water into the eggs. Pour into a medium skillet over medium heat. Cook until it gets thicker. Take it off the heat & slice it into strips.

4. In a medium sauce-pan over medium-high heat, heat the vegetable oil. Slowly cook the onion & stir it until it is soft.

Mix in the beef & 1 tbsp of soy sauce & cook until the meat is evenly brown. Drain & put away.

5. Set oven temperature to 350°F. (175°C). Put the nori sheets on a medium baking sheet & heat them for 1 to 2-min in an oven that has been preheated until they are slightly crisp.

6. Put each sheet of nori on a bamboo rolling mat one at a time. Line the nori sheets evenly with about ¾-inch (2 cm) of rice, being careful not to cover the edges of the nori with rice. Starting at one end of the nori sheet, put a carrot stick, a line of tuna, chard, an egg, a slice of cucumber & a line of beef on top of the rice. Repeat this process until the food is about halfway up the nori sheet. The sheets need to be rolled carefully & tightly. Use one or two grains of the sticky rice to make a seal. Cut each roll into about four pieces each & serve.

Mackerel Pressed Sushi (Saba Oshisushi)

Prep Time: 40 mins
Cook Time: 40 mins
Overall: 1 hr 20 mins
Servings: 2
Calories (Per Serving): 764

Ingredients

6 shsio leaves
2 rice cooker cups of uncooked Japanese short-grain rice (2x180ml= 360 ml; 300 g)
4 tbsp of Kikkoman* Seasoned Rice Vinegar (or homemade sushi vinegar)
1 frozen marinated mackerel fillet (shime saba) (defrosted in the fridge overnight)
- Homemade Sushi Vinegar Seasonings
4 tbsp rice vinegar (unseasoned)
2 tbsp of sugar
1 tsp kosher salt (Diamond Crystal; use ½ for table salt)

Instructions

1. Get all of the ingredients together.
- To Prepare Sushi Rice

1. Use a rice cooker cup to measure the rice, then rinse it under cold water by gently rubbing it in a circle with your fingers. Put the rice in water & pour out the water that has starch in it. Rinse & do this again & again until the water is clear.

2. Soak the rice for 20 to 30-min in water.

3. Drain all of the water & wait for 10-min. If you don't have time to wait, try to shake off as much water as possible. The rice should be put into the rice cooker.

4. Pour enough water to make 2 cups of "Sushi Rice" (or a little less than 2 cups if you don't have "Sushi Rice") & start cooking. If you don't have a rice cooker, get 360 ml of water ready (we use less water than regular rice because the rice will be seasoned after it's cooked) & follow my instructions for cooking rice in the Instant Pot or in a pot on the stove.

5. When the rice is done cooking, use a rice scoop or paddle to fluff it. Wet a sushi oke/hangiri (a round wooden tub with a flat bottom) or a big bowl with water, so the rice doesn't stick. Spread the cooked rice out evenly in the sushi oke so it will cool down faster.

6. While the rice is still hot, mix in 4 tbsp of Kikkoman* Seasoned Rice Vinegar or sushi vinegar that you made yourself. Add more or less varying on your taste. Instead of mixing the rice, use a rice paddle to cut it at a 45-degree angle. In the meantime, you need to cool the rice with a fan so that it shines & doesn't get too soft.

7. Then, flip the rice gently every few slices. Keep doing this until the rice has cooled down. Cover the rice with a wet towel or paper towel until you are ready to use it.

- To Prepare Mackerel

1. Open the defrosted mackerel fillet that had been marinated & cut it in half along its length.

2. Make a butterfly shape with the fillet from the long edge you just cut. If you want to see more, please watch the video. Do the other half again.

3. [Optional] Put the two pieces on a ceramic plate & use a kitchen torch to lightly sear the skin to give it a nice char flavor.

- To Make Pressed Sushi

1. Add 1 tbsp of Kikkoman* Seasoned Rice Vinegar to 1 tbsp of water in a small bowl (or rice vinegar). So, the rice doesn't stick to your hands, wet them.

2. Put the bottom base & side of the Oshibako mold together so that the top is open. Use the vinegar water to wet it, so the rice doesn't stick to it.

3. First, put the skin side of the mackerel fillet on the bottom. If the fillet is bigger than the box, cut off the extra & fill any gaps.

4. Then, put shiso leaves on top of the mackerel.

5. From one side to the other, add rice. Fill the corners with rice using your fingers & try to keep the amount of rice the same everywhere.

6. If you need to, add more rice & fill the mold to just above the rim.

7. Put the mold's top piece in place & use it to press down hard on the rice.

8. Turn 180 degrees & use your body weight to press down again.

9. Turn the mold over so the piece that was on top is now on the bottom. Slide the mold's side wall down.

10. Take off the top part. Use a knife to separate the fish from the top piece if it is stuck. Put the bottom piece through the sidewall & push it up.

11. The finished oshisushi is now on the piece at the bottom. Put a knife in to separate the top piece from the bottom.

12. Cut each half of the oshisushi into three pieces. Place on a plate & add some pickled ginger as a garnish. You can do this again for another mackerel. Before making the second batch, clean the mold & wet it. You can also use plastic wrap to avoid cleaning it every time.

- What to do with leftover Sushi Rice?

1. For quick sushi, you can make Temari Sushi or Hand Roll Sushi. You can also freeze up to one month.

- Equipment

Oshibako (Sushi Press)

Mexican Sushi

Servings: 6
Yields: 6 servings
Calories (Per Serving): 333

Ingredients

3 -oz low-fat cream cheese, softened
1 ½ tbsp seeded & finely chopped chipotle in adobo
1 large plain flour tortilla
1 large tomato-flavored tortilla
1 large spinach-flavored tortilla
¾ cup low-fat refried black beans
6 tbsp Pico de Gallo salsa
1 ½ Avocado from Mexico, peeled, pitted & diced
¾ cup chopped cilantro leaves

Instructions

1. Mix cream cheese & chipotle together. To soften tortillas, you can heat them in a microwave or oven. Spread 2 tbsp of chipotle cream cheese, ¼ cup of black beans & 2 tbsp of salsa on each tortilla. Spread one-third of the avocado & cilantro on each.

2. Wrap tortillas tightly in plastic wrap & put them in the fridge. To serve, take the rolls out of their wrapping & cut off the ends. Then, cut each roll across into six pieces.

Mini Cucumber Sushi Rolls

Prep Time: 30 mins
Overall: 30 mins
Servings: 12
Yields: 24 appetizers
Calories (Per Serving): 46

Ingredients

1 long seedless cucumber, ends trimmed
1 carrot, shredded
1 (4 -oz) package cream cheese, softened
¼ cup raisins
24 long fresh chives for tying

Instructions

1. Using a peeler, cut the cucumber into 8 slices that are ⅛-inch thick & 1-inch long. Cut each slice across the middle into three pieces.

2. Put about 1 tsp of shredded carrot on the bottom edge of a cucumber slice. Top the carrot with about 1 tsp of cream cheese & 2 or 3 raisins. Starting at the filled end, roll the cucumber slice into a little sushi roll. Tie the roll shut with a chive. Do this with the rest of the ingredients.

Miso-Marinated Hamachi Bowl

Prep Time: 10 mins
Cook Time: 5 mins
Marinate Time: 30 mins
Servings: 4
Calories (Per Serving): 145

Ingredients

1 lb. of sashimi-grade yellowtail (Hamachi)
1 knob ginger (1 tsp grated ginger)
- Seasonings

2 tbsp mirin
2 tbsp's sake
4 tbsp soy sauce (gluten-free soy sauce for GF)
2 tbsp miso
- Garnish

10 shiso leaves (perilla/ooba)
1 green onion/scallion
¼ tsp toasted white sesame seeds
sushi ginger (gari) (optional)

Instructions

1. Gather up all the ingredients together.
- To Make the Marinade:

1. Ginger should be peeled & grated. About 1 tsp of grated ginger will be needed.

2. Mix mirin, sake & soy sauce in a small sauce-pan.

3. Bring it to a simmer over medium heat & let the alcohol evaporate for a-min. Then take it off the heat & stir in the miso.

4. Whisk the miso & the sauce together. Then add the grated ginger & stir everything together. Set aside.
- To cut Hamachi:

1. Cut the Hamachi into 5 mm slices with a sharp sashimi knife.
- To Marinate Hamachi:

1. Put some marinade in the bottom of a deep glass container with a lid & start layering the Hamachi slices. Then pour the marinade over the meat.

2. Add more Hamachi slices & then pour the marinade on top.

3. When you're done slicing the Hamachi, close the lid & put it in the fridge for 30-min to 2-hours (2 hrs maximum; otherwise, it gets salty).
- To Prepare Hamachi Bowl:

1. Finely slice the green onion/scallion.

2. The shiso leaves need to be washed & dried with a paper towel. The shiso leaves are rolled up. Some of the shisos should be kept for serving.

3. Cut the shiso leaves into thin strips & spread them out.

4. Set aside steamed rice bowls so it stays cool. Get the Hamachi sashimi out of the fridge & prepare the toppings. On top of the rice, put the shiso.

5. Put the slices of sashimi on top of the rice. Add sesame seeds, green onion, shiso chiffonade & sushi ginger to the top. Enjoy!

Mom's Sushi Rice

Prep Time: 10 mins
Cook Time: 20 mins
Extra Time: 35 mins
Overall: 1 hrs 5 mins
Servings: 10
Yields: 5 cups
Calories (Per Serving): 181

Ingredients

2 ¼ cups Japanese sushi-style rice
1 (4-inch) piece konbu dried kelp (Not mandatory)
3 cups water
¼ cup rice vinegar
¼ cup white sugar
1 ¼ tsp salt

Instructions

1. Put the rice in a deep, large bowl. Fill with cold water & use your hands to rub the rice together until the water turns milky white. Carefully pour out cloudy water without spilling the rice. Repeat 3 or 4 times until you can see the rice through 3-inches of water.

2. Drain the rice in fine strainer & then add it, the konbu & 3 cups of water to a pot. Give it 30-min to sit. In a small bowl, mix the rice vinegar, sugar & salt until the sugar & salt are dissolved. Set aside.

3. Cover the rice & bring it to boil with high heat. Then turn down the heat to low & let it cook for 15-min. Take it off the heat & let it sit for 5-min with the lid on.

4. Scrap the rice into a bowl. Take out the konbu & throw it away. Stir in the vinegar mixture until the rice is smooth & there are no more lumps. Let the temperature drop to room temperature. To cool the rice quickly & make it look better, use an electric fan.

Mosaic Sushi

Prep Time: 40 mins
Overall: 40 mins
Servings: 3
Calories (Per Serving): 465

Ingredients

- For the Sushi Rice

2 tbsp of sugar

3½ cups of cooked Japanese short-grain rice (2 rice cooker cups (2 x 180ml= 360ml or 300g) of uncooked Japanese short-grain rice yield 3½ US cups (660 g) of cooked rice)

4 tbsp of rice vinegar (unseasoned)

1 tsp of kosher salt (Diamond Crystal; use ½ for table salt)

- For Garnishes (not mandatory)

1 okra (blanched; need a slice or two)

yuzu zest (can use lemon zest)

kinome leaves (can use a tiny parsley leaf)

chives

tobiko (flying fish roe)

edible gold leaf flakes

1 slice of lemon

- For the Toppings

3 slices of sashimi-grade salmon

3 slices of sashimi-grade tuna (I used *otoro*)

6 pieces of sashimi-grade shrimp (amaebi)

2 snap peas

2 pieces of cooked shrimp

1 piece of sashimi-grade scallop

2 pieces of cooked surf clam (hokkigai)

4 tbsp of Ikura (save some for garnish)

1 Tamagoyaki (Sweet Rolled Omelet) (need a few thin slices)

1 Japanese or Persian cucumber (need a few slices)

1 red radish (thinly sliced)

2 tbsp of green peas (blanched)

Instructions

- Before Cooking

1. Gather up all the ingredients together. For the Mosaic Sushi, it helps to use a ruler to make a precise checkerboard pattern.

- To Make the Sushi Rice

1. To make sushi vinegar (sushizu), put the rice vinegar, sugar & salt in a small sauce-pan & bring it to a boil with medium heat. Mix until all of the sugar has dissolved. You can also place the ingredients in a bowl that can go in the microwave & heat it for 1-min, or until the sugar is dissolved. Put it away to let it cool down.

2. If you're using a wooden sushi oke, which is also called a "hangiri," wet it with running water & let it dry well. A baking sheet can also be used. Move the rice that has been cooked into the sushi oke. Spread the rice out so it will cool more quickly.

3. Sprinkle the rice with the sushi vinegar.

4. Gently "slice" the rice at a 45-degree angle with a rice paddle to mix in the sushi vinegar mixture & separate the pieces of rice. Don't stir or mix the rice, or the grains might break & the rice will get mushy. If your rice is freshly cooked, use a paddle fan or another type of fan to blow

hard on it while you slice it. This cools the rice & gets rid of any extra water. The rice gets shiny & doesn't get mushy when it's fanned. Flip the rice with care between each slice. Repeat this process until the rice is as cool as a person's skin.

5. The sesame seeds should be sprinkled on top & then employing a motion similar to slicing should be distributed evenly throughout the sushi rice. Set aside.

- To Pack the Sushi Rice

1. Put a piece of parchment paper on bottom of your container. Here, I'm using a Japanese lacquered box called a jubako that is 7 ½-inches by 7 ½-inches (19 cm by 19 cm). This box is used for Osechi Ryori or lunch box. If you don't line the container with parchment paper, the rice will stick to the bottom, making it hard to pick up each piece of sushi.

2. Put the sushi rice that has already been made into the container. The measured amount of rice, which is the whole 2 cups you cooked in the rice cooker, is just right for this standard jubako size. Use the rice paddle to spread the sushi rice evenly to the container's corners & edges & make sure the bed of sushi rice is leveled.

3. Wet a plastic dough scraper with water & then use it to press the sushi rice down firmly. We don't want to press the rice too hard & break up the grains, but the rice should be packed tightly so that the sushi cubes keep their shape when you pick them up.

4. Press the sushi rice down more & more with the dough scraper. Don't forget to wet it so the rice does not stick to it. Since this kind of sushi is called oshisushi, which means "pressed," it is normal to press the rice grains.

5. Now, make squares or cubes out of the sushi rice. Put some water on the dough scraper & use it to make a series of cuts across the sushi box's width through the sushi rice bed. The slices should be evenly distance apart so that the checkerboard pattern will have neat squares. Measure your sushi box so that each slice is about 1 ¼-inches (3 cm) to 1 ½-inches (4 cm) away from the next. I cut the sushi rice about 1 ⅓-inches (3.5 cm) wide for my 7 ½-inch x 7 ½-inch (19cm x 19cm) container. Wet the scraper after every cut to keep it from sticking.

6. Then, turn the container 90 degrees & make more cuts across the width of the box that are evenly distance apart as the first cuts (1 ⅓-inches or 3.5 cm in my case). You now have square cubes that are about 1 ⅓-inches (3.5 cm) in size. Set aside.

7. Go over your slices a-sec time to separate & squeeze the squares of sushi even more. This will likely to make it easier to pull out each cube when serving. Start by putting the clean, wet dough scraper into the first slice you made earlier. Move the scraper back & forth along the length of the slice in a sawing motion to make sure the two sides are clearly separated. Then, press the scraper along the right side to pack the rice in tightly. Continue down the left side. Now there will be about 1 mm of space between the two sides. Repeat this "separate & compress" process with the next slice. Between slices, wet the scraper with water & wipe it clean of any rice grains or leftovers. Keep going until you've cut all of the slices lengthwise in that direction. Then turn the container 90 degrees & do the same thing with the other slices.

- To Prepare the Toppings

  1. Start by cutting your topping ingredients into squares that are slightly bigger than your sushi cubes. I made mine about 3.6 cm wide for my 3.5 cm sushi cubes.

  2. Tip: If you want your sushi to look its best, cut the toppings a little bigger than cube size so that they cover the sushi rice completely & there are no gaps you can see. I use a vegetable peeler to make paper-thin strips out of the cucumber. Pile up three or four ribbons & cut them into squares that are 3.6 cm by 3.6 cm.

  3. Put the knife into the pods of the snap peas to open them. Cut them into pieces that are 3.6 cm wide & 3.6 cm long.

  4. Cut the blanched okra into ⅛-inch (3 mm) thick rounds. Cut the Tamagoyaki into ⅛-inch (3 mm) slices, then cut each slice into a 3.6 cm square.

  5. Try your hardest to make a square shape with the sashimi. Here, I cut one slice of salmon sashimi in half & stacked it in a way that looks like a square.

  6. Cut the scallop in half across the middle to make each piece thinner. For the cooked surf clams (hokkigai), cut each one in ½ & then cut each half into four squares.

- To Decorate the Mosaic Sushi

  1. Put one kind of topping on each square of the Mosaic Sushi to decorate it. Make sure the lines of the checkerboard pattern stay straight & that the toppings cover all of the sushi rice. As you place the toppings, think about the color, texture & direction of each one. For example, don't put ingredients that are the same color next to each other. Use a small garnish like ikura, tobiko, the zest of a citrus fruit, or an herb to add depth.

- To Serve

  1. You can dip Mosaic Sushi in soy sauce & wasabi. Serve green tea & sushi ginger (gari) that has been pickled on the side.

- For Storing:

  1. You can put the remaining in the fridge for 24-hours if you cover them with plastic wrap. Fish that is good for sashimi should be eaten within 24–36-hours of buying it.

Nigiri Sushi

Prep Time: 1 hrs
Cook Time: 35 mins
Extra Time: 30 mins
Overall: 2 hrs 5 mins
Servings: 4
Yields: 4
Calories (Per Serving): 555

Ingredients

4 cups water
2 cups uncooked white rice
½ cup seasoned rice vinegar
1 tsp white sugar, or as needed
1 tsp salt, or as needed
¼ pound Hamachi (yellowtail)
¼ pound maguro (tuna)
¼ pound cooked Ebi (shrimp), shelled & butterflied
6 eggs
½ tsp white sugar
⅛ tsp salt
1 tsp wasabi paste (Optional)
1 sheet nori, cut into 1-inch strips

Instructions

1. In a pot with high heat, bring the water & rice to a boil. Turn the heat down to medium-low, cover & simmer for 20 to 25-min, or until the rice is soft & the liquid is gone. Place the rice in a bowl & use a rice paddle or a wooden spoon to mix in the rice vinegar. Add a tsp of sugar & a tsp of salt, or more or less according to your taste. Give it about 30-min to cool to room temperature.

2. Cut the fish into thin pieces about 2-inches long & 1-inch wide by cutting across the grain. Keep it in the fridge until ready to use.

3. In a bowl, whisk together eggs, ½ tsp of sugar & ¼ tsp of salt. About a quarter of the mixture should be spread out thinly in a large, greased skillet over medium heat. Cook without stirring for about 2 to 3-min, or until the food is done. Roll into a log & place it on one side of the pan. Repeat with ¼ of the egg mixture, rolling each log into a new one to make one big one. Cut the omelet into pieces about ½-inch thick & on the diagonal.

4. Put a piece of fish or shrimp in your hand & a small amount of wasabi paste on it, if you want to. Grab one to two tbsp of rice & roll it into a small nugget in your hand. Put the rice ball on top of the fish or shrimp & gently press down on it, so it sticks. Set aside while you put the rest of the fish & shrimp together.

5. Take a piece of egg omelet in one hand & 1 to 2 tbsp of rice in the other. Roll the egg omelet & rice into a small ball in your hand. Put the rice ball on top of the egg & gently press down on it to make it stick.

6. Wrap each package with a strip of nori. Moisten one end of the nori strip & press it together to seal.

Otoro Sushi Two Ways

Prep Time: 10 mins
Overall: 10 mins
Calories (Per Serving): 109

Ingredients

sushi-grade otoro (fatty tuna)
sushi rice pillows
yuzu
- For Serving:

soy sauce
wasabi
sushi ginger

Instructions

1. Get all of the ingredients together.

2. Take off the skin & cut the edges.

3. Slice to the thickness you want. Because it has a lot of fat, a thinner slice is best.

4. Remove the meat from the skin by scraping it. This part is thought to be the best parts of a tuna & it can be used to make negitoro donburi.

5. Sear the otoro with a kitchen blow torch to bring out the hidden umami flavors.

6. Place the seared otoro on the sushi pillows & drizzle yuzu juice on top. Use soy sauce, wasabi & sushi ginger to top the food.

PBJ Sushi Kids Bento Box

Prep Time: 15 mins
Overall: 15 mins
Servings: 1
Yields: 1 bento box
Calories (Per Serving): 494

Ingredients

1 (8-inch) flour tortilla
peanut butter
1 tbsp grape jelly, or to taste
1 banana, sliced
1 ½ tbsp chocolate syrup, or to taste

Instructions

1. The tortilla should be covered in jelly on one half & peanut butter on the other. Start rolling the tortilla from the side with the jelly & seal it. Slice into sushi roll-sized pieces. Place the banana & chocolate syrup (the "ginger" & "soy sauce") in separate compartments of a bento box & serve.

- Notes

You can use jelly of any flavor you like.
This recipe could be made with either white or whole wheat tortillas.
You can use light or sugar-free chocolate syrup instead of the regular kind.

Perfect Sushi Rice

Prep Time: 5 mins
Cook Time: 20 mins
Overall: 25 mins
Servings: 15
Yields: 5 cups
Calories (Per Serving): 112

Ingredients

2 cups of uncooked glutinous white rice (sushi rice)
½ cup rice vinegar
1 tbsp vegetable oil
¼ cup white sugar
1 tsp salt
3 cups of water

Instructions

1. Run cold water over the rice in a strainer or colander until water runs clear.

2. Mix rice & water in a pot & bring to a boil over medium-high heat. Turn the heat down to low, cover & cook for about 20-min, or until the rice is soft & all the water has been absorbed. Take it off the stove & put it somewhere else until it's cool enough to handle.

3. In the meantime, mix rice vinegar, oil, sugar & salt in a small sauce-pan over medium heat. Cook until the sugar is completely gone. Let it cool, then mix it into the rice that has been cooked. At first, the mixture will look very wet, but as you stir it, the rice will dry out as it cools.

Philadelphia Roll

Prep Time: 20 mins
Overall: 20 mins
Servings: 1 roll
Calories (Per Serving): 285

Ingredients

1 nori sheet
½ cup prepared sushi rice
¼ avocado, sliced
2 oz smoked salmon, sliced
2 tbsp cream cheese

Instructions

1. Spread the sushi rice out evenly on the nori sheet, leaving about a 1-inch border around the edges.

2. Lay the avocado & salmon slices out flat on bottom ½ of rice.

3. Cover salmon & avocado slices with cream cheese.

4. For a tight seal, roll the nori sheet away from you & up it.

5. Put roll on a cutting board & use a clean sharp knife to cut it into 6 to 8 pieces.

6. Add soy sauce right away & serve. Enjoy!

Pickled Sushi Ginger (Gari)

Prep Time: 15 mins
Cook Time: 5 mins
Pickling Time: 4 hrs
Overall: 4 hrs 20 mins
Servings: 1
Calories (Per Serving): 268

Ingredients

8 oz young ginger (you can increase the ginger by as much as 50% for this recipe; regular ginger will be very spicy, but you can use it if you increase the boiling time to reduce the spiciness)
2 tsp of kosher salt (Diamond Crystal; use ½ for table salt) (for sprinkling, 3–5% of the ginger's weight)
- For the Sweet Vinegar (Amazu)
1 tsp kosher salt (Diamond Crystal; use ½ for table salt)
1 cup rice vinegar, unseasoned (rice vinegar is milder than other vinegars; if you use a different kind, add more sugar to adjust the flavor).
½–¾ cup sugar (I used organic cane sugar, but white granulated sugar will make a clear pickling solution that shows off the pink color better; DO NOT USE LESS SUGAR THAN DIRECTED because the ginger won't keep well; ½ cup is the least you can use & it's still quite sour; if you like the taste of store-bought sushi ginger, use the higher measurement of sugar indicated)

Instructions

1. Get all of the ingredients together.
- To Prepare the Ginger
1. Use a knife (or the back of the knife or a spoon) to scrape off the ginger's brown spots & thin skin.
2. Using a peeler, cut the ginger into thin slices. A mandolin can also be used. I like to use a peeler because it makes thin slices.
3. When you can't slice any more ginger with the peeler/mandolin, use the knife to thinly slice what's left.

4. Salt the ginger slices & leave them alone for 5-min. The salt helps take the water out of the ginger so that it can soak up the pickling solution better.

5. In the meantime, boil a medium pot of water. When the water starts to boil, blanch the thinly sliced ginger for 1 to 2-min. If you want it to be spicy, take it out after 1 ½-min. If you're using regular ginger instead of young ginger, boil it for 2 to 3-min to get rid of the extra heat.

6. Using a sieve, drain the ginger slices. Let them cool down just a bit so you can handle them.

7. Spread the slices out in a single layer on a sizable Japanese bamboo sieve (called bonzaru) or a paper towel/wire rack using clean hands. Put it away until it's completely cooled down & a little bit drier.

8. Once the ginger slices have cooled, squeeze the liquid out of them & put them in a clean, airtight jar.
- To Make the Sweet Vinegar (Amazu)
1. Put the rice vinegar, sugar & salt in a small saucepan.

2. Mix it up & bring it to a boil in medium heat. Cook

the vinegar mixture until the strong smell of vinegar is gone & all of the sugar has dissolved.

3. Take it off from the heat & then let it cool down a bit, because the liquid that just boiled could break the glass jar. Put the ginger slices in the jar. Then pour the hot vinegar mixture on top. Mix it well with clean chopsticks (or any other tool). Close the lid, let it cool all the way down & put it in the fridge.

4. After about 4-hours, the ginger will start to turn a light pink color. I think you should wait until the next day or a few days after that to enjoy.

- For Storing:

1. Put the pickled ginger in a container that won't let air in & store it in the fridge for up to a year. Always use clean tools to get the pickled ginger out of the jar. This will keep it from getting dirty & help it last for a long time.

Poke Bowl

Prep Time: 15 mins
Overall: 15 mins
Servings: 3
Calories (Per Serving): 435

Ingredients

- For Seasonings

¼ tsp of kosher salt (Diamond Crystal; use ½ for table salt)

⅓ cup soy sauce (gluten-free soy sauce, or GF soy sauce).

2 tsp of roasted sesame oil

1 tbsp rice vinegar (unseasoned)

1 tbsp of toasted black & white sesame seeds

- For the Poke

½ lb. of sashimi-grade tuna (try Ahi or skipjack for an authentic flavor)

½ lb. sashimi-grade salmon (not traditional in a poke, salmon brings a nice color to dish)

Handful of seaweed limu

2 scallions or green onions

¼ onion

1 tsp of roasted candlenut or kukui nut (inamona) (make sure they are roasted/toasted)

- For the Donburi Bowl

3 servings of cooked Japanese short-grain rice (2½ rice cooker cups (2.5x180ml = 450 ml) of uncooked rice makes about three servings (five US cups) of cooked rice for donburi)

Instructions

1. Get all of the ingredients together.

2. Cut the fresh salmon & tuna that are good for sashimi into bite-sized pieces. I think the texture will be better if you cut them into slightly bigger pieces.

3. If you want to use the limu, wash it well & cut it into pieces that are about ½-inch long (1.3 cm). Cut the green onions into thin slices.

4. Cut the onion into pieces that are ¾-inches long & 2 cm wide.

5. Put the salmon & tuna in a large bowl & sprinkle the kosher salt or Hawaiian sea salt on top. Then, add cut onions, sliced green onions, chopped limu (optional) & roasted kukui nuts (optional) to the bowl.

6. To the bowl, add the soy sauce, sesame oil & rice vinegar. Sprinkle the white & black sesame seeds that have been toasted on top & gently mix everything together. You can cover it & put it in the fridge up to 12-hours early.

- To Serve

1. Use a large donburi bowl or plate to serve the steamed rice. Let it cool down for a while. Then pile on the poke. You can add whatever mix-ins or toppings you want (see Notes below). Serve & eat right away.

- For Storing:

1. It's best to eat it in the same day you bought it. The poke ingredients can be kept in the fridge for about 24-hours. I think you should cook the rice right before you serve it.

Toppings Ideas:

- Avocado: The avocado's richness makes it taste like fatty tuna & gives it a creamy texture.

- Veggies like cucumbers, radishes & carrots. Based on what you use, you can always thinly slice or dice the veggies into fun shapes to add color & a refreshing crunch.
- Edamame is a good source of protein & gives the dish a nice texture.
- Microgreens, like daikon sprouts, broccoli sprouts & kale sprouts, are beautiful & full of nutrients.
- Cherry tomatoes, cut in fourths; ripe tomatoes add sweetness, flavor & a touch of acidity.
- Masago are tiny, salty fish eggs that give a dish a pop of color & an interesting taste.
- Seaweed: Shredded nori or julienned seaweed give the poke bowl a crispy texture.
- Sesame seeds make the bowl smell nutty & good & make the dish look nice.
- Macadamia nuts are mild & creamy. When they are roasted & chopped, they taste a bit like roasted kukui nuts.
- Furikake (rice seasonings) is a fun & tasty addition.
- The recipe for pickled sushi ginger is cool & tangy.
- Wasabi – so good with fresh sashimi.
- Spicy Mayo: You only need Japanese mayonnaise & sriracha sauce to make this delicious sauce. It will add a creamy, spicy kick to your poke bowl.

Quick & Easy Chirashi Sushi

Prep Time: 20 mins
Cook Time: 1 hr
Overall: 1 hr 20 mins
Servings: 3
Calories (Per Serving): 344

Ingredients

- For Toppings

kinshi tamago (shredded egg crepe)

ikura (salmon roe)

snow peas (blanched)

shredded nori seaweed (kizami nori)

- For Chirashi Sushi

About two rice cooker cups of uncooked Japanese short-grain rice (2 rice cooker cups (2 x 180ml = 360ml) yields about 4 servings (3 ½ US cups)

400 ml water.

1 packet of chirashi sushi mix

Instructions

1. Gather up all the ingredients together. You can use a rice cooker, an Instant Pot, or a pot on stove to cook 2 cups of rice. While the rice is cooking, make Kinshi Tamago.

2. Put cooked rice in a large salad bowl or baking sheet. (You can buy a Hangiri or Sushi Oke on Amazon.) My hangiri is 10-inches (26 cm) long, which is large enough for a family of **4**. While the rice is still hot, add one package of Chirashi Sushi Mix.

3. Everything should be put together. Instead of "mixing," use a rice paddle to slice through the grains to separate them.

4. Snow pea, ikura (salmon roe) & Kinshi Tamago are used as garnishes when served in a bowl or plate. You can put whatever you want on top, like your favorite sashimi. Sprinkle shredded nori.

- For Storing:

1. Rice gets hard when it's stored in the fridge, so it's best to cover it with plastic wrap & a thick kitchen towel.

Rainbow Roll

Prep Time: 30 mins
Overall: 30 mins
Servings: 1 roll
Calories (Per Serving): 325

Ingredients

1 nori sheet
½ cup prepared sushi rice
¼ avocado, sliced
1 oz crabstick, sliced
¼ cucumber, sliced
Assorted raw fish slices

Instructions

1. Spread out sushi rice out evenly on a sheet of nori, leaving about a 1-inch border around the top.

2. Put the avocado, cucumber & crabsticks in a row across the bottom half of the rice.

3. Put rainbow-colored slices of different kinds of raw fish on top.

4. Roll the nori sheet up straight away from you to seal the fillings.

5. Put roll on a cutting board & then use a very clean & sharp knife to cut it into 6 to 8 pieces.

6. Add soy sauce right away & serve.

Sarah's Special Sushi

Prep Time: 30 mins
Cook Time: 20 mins
Servings: 2
Yields: 12 pieces
Calories (Per Serving): 787

Ingredients

2 sheets nori (dry seaweed)
1 cup uncooked medium-grain white rice
1 ¼ cups water
1 ½ tbsp rice vinegar
1 ½ tbsp white sugar
1 pinch salt
3 -oz cold cream cheese, cut into thin strips & divided
2 tsp crushed garlic, divided
½ cup crushed cashews, divided
2 green onions, finely chopped, divided
2 -oz smoked salmon, cut into strips & divided
soy sauce
wasabi pastes

Instructions

1. Once the rinse water is nearly clear, repeat the process many times with fresh rice & then thoroughly drain. Put the rice & 1¼ cups water in a large pot with a lid. Bring the water to boil & then turn down heat to low & cover the pot. Simmer the rice for 15 to 20-min, or until the water has been soaked up & the top of the rice looks dry. Take the rice off the heat & let it steam for another 20-min while it is covered.

2. With a wooden spoon, mix the rice vinegar, sugar & salt into the rice. Spread the rice out on a metal sheet pan to cool.

3. Set the oven temperature to 350°F. (175°C).

4. To soften the first sheet of nori, put it in the oven for 4-min. Remove & put the shiny side down on a bamboo mat that has been wrapped in plastic. The longer side should be facing left to right. (It's unnecessary, but the wrap helps keep things clean.) Wet your hands & then press a layer of the rice onto the nori by leaving ½-inch of space on the side closest to you & 1-inch on the side farthest away. It should be about ½-inch thick & as flat as possible.

5. Place half of the cream cheese slices in a line down the very center of the sheet. Add ½ tsp of garlic, ½ cup of crushed cashews & ½ cup of spring onions. Set half of the smoked salmon strips on top of the cream cheese.

6. Grab the edge of the bamboo rolling sheet. Now, fold the bottom edge up to cover the filling & roll the sushi tightly into a cylinder. Brush a line of water along the last edge of the nori sheet, then roll & press the sheet to seal it. Once the sushi is rolled, place it on the mat & squeeze it gently to make it tight. Do the same thing with the-sec nori sheet & the rest of the fillings.

7. Use a sharp, wet knife to cut each roll into six pieces. Have a damp paper towel handy to wipe off any leftovers & wet the blade with water before each cut. Serve with wasabi paste & soy sauce.

Scallop Sushi

Prep Time: 10 mins
Overall: 10 mins
Servings: 2
Calories (Per Serving): 36

Ingredients

2 sushi-grade scallops
⅓ cup sushi rice (cooked & seasoned)
wasabi (optional)

- Tezu (vinegared hand-dipping water):

¼ cup water
2 tsp rice vinegar (unseasoned)

- Toppings (not mandatory):

2 tsp yuzu-flavored tobiko (flying fish roe)
2 tsp Homemade Spicy Mayo
2 chives

Instructions

1. Gather all the ingredients together.

2. Take off the muscle from the scallops.

3. Flip the scallops over.

4. Wet your hands with Tezu (vinegar-dipped hand) & pick up a ball of sushi, the rice about the size of a tbsp. With your right hand, gently squeeze the rice to make a rectangular block with rounded edges that slides. Press down on the rice as you shape it into a solid base for the scallops.

5. Add a little bit of wasabi to each piece of rice, if you like & place a scallop on top of each one. Add tobiko & spicy mayo to each scallop & then put a chive on top. Because scallop is raw, eat them the same day.

Simplified Sushi Vinegar

Prep Time: 5 mins
Cook Time: 10 mins
Overall: 15 mins
Servings: 12
Yields: 2 ¾ cups
Calories (Per Serving): 97

Ingredients

- 2 cups rice vinegar (such as Marukan*)
- 1 ½ cups white sugar
- 1 ½ tbsp salt
- ⅛ lemon, juiced

Instructions

1. In a sauce-pan, mix rice vinegar, sugar, salt & lemon juice over low heat until the sugar & salt dissolve. Do not let the mixture boil.

2. Take it off the heat & let it cool all the way down. Put them in the fridge.

Sesame Seared Tuna & Sushi Bar Spinach

Prep Time: 15 mins
Cook Time: 5 mins
Servings: 2
Yields: 2 servings
Calories (Per Serving): 593

Ingredients

- For Miso Mayo Sauce:
¼ cup mayonnaise
2 tsp white miso paste
1 tbsp seasoned rice vinegar
- For Seared Tuna:
2 (5 -oz) sushi-grade ahi tuna steaks
salt to taste
2 tbsp black sesame seeds
2 tsp vegetable oil
1 tbsp prepared ponzu sauce
- For Spinach Salad:
½ pound baby spinach leaves
3 tbsp white sesame seeds
1 tbsp white sugar
1 tbsp soy sauce, or to taste
½ tsp mirin

Instructions

1. Put the spinach in a dry pot over medium-high heat & stir it until it just starts to wilt, which will take about 1 to 2-min. Put in a strainer to cool down.

2. While the spinach is cooling, toast the white sesame seeds in a dry pan with medium heat until they are light golden brown. Use a mortar & pestle to crush the mixture into a very coarse paste, leaving some of the seeds whole. White sugar, soy sauce & mirin should be added. Mix everything together with a wooden spoon & set aside.

3. Put the spinach that has cooled down on a towel & squeeze out any extra liquid. Chop things up roughly & put them in a bowl. Mix well after adding the sauce. Before serving, cover & chill thoroughly.

4. To make miso mayo sauce, mix together mayonnaise, miso paste & rice vinegar. Put it in fridge until you need it.

5. Lightly salt tuna steaks, then sprinkle with as many sesame seeds as desired while lightly pressing them.

6. Oil a pan that doesn't stick & put it over medium heat. Sear the tuna steaks for 30 to 45-sec on each side & along each edge in a hot pan.

7. Slice the tuna & put it on top of the miso sauce. Tuna is served with a spinach salad on the side & is brushed with ponzu.

- Notes
If you want, you can add some toasted sesame oil to the spinach. You can use white sesame seeds instead of black ones for the tuna.
After being seared, the tuna can be put in the fridge to cool down. It can also be served cold.

Smoked Salmon Sushi Roll

Prep Time: 30 mins
Extra Time: 4 hrs 30 mins
Overall: 5 hrs
Servings: 6
Yields: 6 rolls
Calories (Per Serving): 291

Ingredients

2 cups Japanese sushi rice

6 tbsp rice wine vinegar

6 sheets nori (dry seaweed)

1 avocado - peeled, pitted & sliced

1 cucumber, peeled & sliced

8 -oz smoked salmon, cut into long strips

2 tbsp wasabi paste

Instructions

1. Let the rice soak for four-hours. Drain the rice & cook it with about 2 cups of water in a rice cooker. Since vinegar will be added later, the rice needs to be a little bit dry.

2. Mix 6 tbsp of rice vinegar into the hot rice as soon as it is done cooking. Spread the rice out on a plate & let it cool completely.

3. Put one sheet of seaweed on a bamboo mat & spread a thin layer of cool rice over it. Leave at least ½-inch of the seaweed uncovered on the top & bottom. This will make it easier to seal later. Wasabi goes well with rice. Put cucumber, avocado & smoked salmon on the rice in a pretty way. Put them about an-inch away from the seaweed's bottom edge.

4. Wet the top edge of the seaweed just a little bit. With the help of the bamboo mat, roll tight from the bottom edge to the top edge. Slice the roll into eight even pieces & serve. Do this with the other rolls.

Spam Musubi

Prep Time: 25 mins
Cook Time: 30 mins
Extra Time: 4 hrs 30 mins
Overall: 5 hrs 25 mins
Servings: 10
Yields: 10 pieces
Calories (Per Serving): 276

Ingredients

2 cups uncooked short-grain white rice
2 cups water
6 tbsp rice vinegar
½ cup white sugar
¼ cup soy sauce
¼ cup oyster sauce
1 (12 -oz) container of fully cooked luncheon meat (such as Spam)
2 tbsp vegetable oil
5 sheets of sushi nori (dry seaweed)

Instructions

1. Soak the rice for 4-hours in enough water to cover it, then drain & rinse.

2. Bring about 2 cups of water to boil in a medium sauce-pan. Stir the rice in. Turn down the heat, cover it & let it cook for 20-min.

3. Take the pan off the heat & add rice vinegar while stirring. Set aside to cool.

4. In a medium bowl, stir together the sugar, soy sauce & oyster sauce until the sugar is completely dissolved. Cut the luncheon meat lengthwise into 10 slices, or to the thickness you want & marinate it in the sauce for 5-min.

5. In a large pan over medium-high heat, heat the oil. About 2-min on each side will give the slices a light brown color.

6. Half the nori sheets & lay them out on a flat surface. Put a rice press in the center of a sheet of paper & pack rice inside it tightly. Place a slice of luncheon meat on top & then take the press away. Wrap rice in nori & seal off the edges with a little bit of water. (You can also shape rice by hand into slices of meat that are about an inch thick.)

7. Musubi can be served hot or cold.

Sauces & Mayo

Spicy Sushi Dipping Sauce

Prep Time: 5 mins
Overall: 5 mins
Servings: 2
Yields: 2 servings
Calories (Per Serving): 17

Ingredients

2 tbsp soy sauce
½ tsp chile-garlic sauce (such as Sriracha*)
¼ tsp sesame oil
1 pinch of garlic powder
1 thin slice of lemon

Instructions

1. Mix soy sauce, chili-garlic sauce, sesame oil, garlic powder & a slice of lemon in a small bowl.

Spicy Sushi Mayo

Prep Time: 5 mins
Overall: 5 mins
Servings: 2
Yields: 2 ½ tbsp
Calories (Per Serving): 107

Ingredients

2 tbsp mayonnaise
2 tsp Sriracha hot sauce
¼ tsp sesame oil

Instructions

1. Using a fork, combine the mayonnaise, Sriracha & sesame oil in a bowl until the mixture is smooth.

Spicy Sushi Roll

Prep Time: 15 mins
Overall: 15 mins
Servings: 3
Yields: 3 rolls
Calories (Per Serving): 341

Ingredients

¼ cup mayonnaise

1 tbsp chile sauce

1 ½ tsp togarashi (Japanese seven spice)

1 tsp prepared wasabi

1 tsp chili powder

1 tsp paprika

3 (3 -oz) fillets of imitation crabmeat, cut into 1 ½-inch piece

2 cups cooked sushi rice

3 sheets nori (dry seaweed)

Instructions

1. In a bowl, combine the mayonnaise, chile sauce, togarashi, wasabi, chili powder & paprika. Stir in the imitation crabmeat until it is evenly coated.

2. Spread an even layer of rice on each sheet of nori. Spoon a row of the crabmeat mixture along the top edge of each sheet of nori. Start on the side with the filling & roll the nori sheet around the crabmeat mixture until it is completely wrapped. Each roll should be cut into 8 equal pieces.

- Notes

If you don't want to use the fake crab, you can use a tuna fillet instead.

Spicy Tuna Sushi Roll

Prep Time: 40 mins
Cook Time: 20 mins
Extra Time: 45 mins
Overall: 1 hrs 45 mins
Servings: 4
Yields: 24 pieces
Calories (Per Serving): 344

Ingredients

2 cups uncooked glutinous white rice

2 ½ cups water

1 tbsp rice vinegar

1 (5 -oz) can of solid white tuna in water, drained

1 tbsp mayonnaise

1 tsp chili powder

1 tsp wasabi paste

4 sheets nori (dry seaweed)

½ cucumber, finely diced

1 carrot, finely diced

1 avocado - peeled, pitted & diced

Instructions

1. In a sauce-pan over high heat, bring the rice, water & vinegar to a boil. Turn the heat down to medium-low, cover & simmer for 20 to 25-min, or until the rice is soft & the liquid is gone. Cover & let it sit for about 10-min to soak up any extra water. Put the rice away to cool down.

2. Mix the tuna, mayonnaise, chili powder & wasabi paste together lightly in a bowl. Break up the tuna, but don't mash it into a paste.

3. To roll the sushi, put plastic wrap over a bamboo sushi rolling mat. Put a sheet of nori on the plastic wrap with the rough side facing up. Put a thick, even layer of cooked rice over the nori & cover it completely by patting it down with wet fingers. Place about 1 tbsp of diced cucumber, carrot & avocado in a line along with the bottom edge of the sheet. Next to the vegetables, spread a line of the tuna mixture.

4. Pick up the edge of the bamboo rolling sheet, then fold the bottom edge up to cover the filling & tightly roll up the sushi into a thick cylinder. Once the sushi is rolled, place it on the mat & squeeze it gently to make it tight. Cut each roll into six pieces & put them in the fridge until ready to serve.

Sushi Cake

Prep Time: 35 mins
Cook Time: 20 mins
Extra Time: 2 hrs
Overall: 2 hrs 55 mins
Servings: 16
Yields: 16
Calories (Per Serving): 353

Ingredients

3 cups medium-grain white rice, uncooked
3 cups water
½ cup rice vinegar
½ cup white sugar
1 tsp salt
1 (8 -oz) package of cream cheese, softened
6 tbsp mayonnaise
2 cups imitation crabmeat
2 cups thinly sliced cucumber
1 medium avocado, thinly sliced
1 (8 -oz) package of cold cream cheese, cut into thin strips
2 tsp sesame seeds, or to taste
1 ½ cups soy sauce
1 medium lime, juiced
2 medium oranges, juiced

Instructions

1. Rinse the rice in cool water until the water is clear & no longer cloudy. Put rice & water in a pot with a lid & bring it to a boil. Cover, turn the heat down to low & simmer for about 15-min, or until the food is soft.

2. In the meantime, put the vinegar, sugar & salt in a sauce-pan & heat it over medium heat until the sugar dissolves. Take it off from the heat & let it cool down.

3. Cream cheese that has been softened & mayonnaise should be put in a blender & mixed until smooth.

4. Cooked rice should be put in a large bowl. Sprinkle about half of the vinegar sauce over the hot rice & mix it together gently. Taste it & if you want, add more vinegar sauce. Pour half of the cooked rice into a springform pan & gently press it down to cover the bottom.

5. Spread half of the mixture of cream cheese & mayonnaise over the rice in the pan. On top, layer crabmeat, cucumber, avocado & cold cream cheese. Spread the rest of the cream cheese & mayonnaise on top. Pour the rest of the rice into the pan & pack it down until the layers are tight. Sprinkle sesame seeds on top. Put in the fridge for at least 2-hours before you serve.

6. Mix soy sauce, orange juice & lime juice. Take the sushi cake out of the springform pan & serve it with the soy sauce.

- Notes

Instead of crab, you can use smoked salmon. I use Calrose rice.

Sushi House Salad Dressing

Prep Time: 10 mins
Overall: 10 mins
Servings: 8
Yields: 1 cup
Calories (Per Serving): 47

Ingredients

3 carrots, peeled & cut in chunks
1 (2-inch) piece fresh ginger root
1 tbsp soy sauce
¼ cup white wine vinegar
¼ cup orange juice
2 tbsp peanut oil

Instructions

1. Blend the carrots, ginger root, soy sauce, vinegar & orange juice in a blender until the mixture is smooth. Pour in the peanut oil & pulse a few times to mix.

Sushi Party

Prep Time: 3 hrs
Cook Time: 30 mins
Overall: 3 hrs 30 mins
Servings: 12
Yields: 12 rolls
Calories (Per Serving): 516

Ingredients

- Rice:

9 ¾ cups water
5 ½ cups Japanese sushi-style white rice
5 ½ tbsp rice vinegar
5 ½ tbsp white sugar
2 ¾ tbsp kosher salt

- Filling:

1 tsp vegetable oil
2 eggs, beaten
1 tbsp vegetable oil
1 tbsp's sake
1 tbsp soy sauce
2 tbsp sesame oil
1 eggplant, sliced lengthwise into strips
1 carrot, sliced into thin strips
1 tbsp rice vinegar
1 tbsp soy sauce
8 spears fresh asparagus
1 avocado
1 tbsp lemon juice, or as needed
12 sheets nori (dry seaweed)
1 (8 -oz) package imitation crabmeat strips, halved lengthwise
1 cucumber, seeded & sliced lengthwise into strips
1 (4 -oz) jar pesto
8 large cooked shrimp, coarsely chopped

Instructions

1. In a large pot, bring water & rice to a boil. Turn the heat down to medium-low, cover & simmer for about 25-min, or until the rice is soft & the liquid has been absorbed. Take off the pot from the heat & then leave the lid on for 10-min.

2. Mix 5 ½ tbsp of rice vinegar, sugar & salt in a bowl that can go in the microwave. Heat for 30 to 45-sec, or until the vinegar mixture is warm. Stir well. Mix the vinegar mixture with the rice & toss it well so that each grain of rice is covered. Let the rice cool completely.

3. In a small pan, heat 1 tsp of vegetable oil over medium heat. Cook eggs in the hot oil for 3 to 5-min, until they are firm. Cut the eggs into strips after putting them on a plate.

4. In a skillet, heat 1 tbsp of vegetable oil, 1 tbsp of soy sauce, 1 tbsp of sake & 1 tbsp of sesame oil over medium heat. Fry eggplant in the oil mixture for 5 to 10-min, until it is soft & has a light char. Place the eggplant on a plate lined with a paper towel.

5. Mix the carrot, a tbsp of rice vinegar & a tbsp of soy sauce in a bowl that can go in the microwave. Microwave for 1 to 2-min, or until the carrot is soft. Drain.

6. Bring a big pot of lightly salted-water to boil &

then add the asparagus. Cook for 2 to 3-min, or until the asparagus is bright green. Drain the asparagus & put it right into a bowl of ice water for a few-min to stop the cooking process. Drain.

7. Cut the avocado into 8 slices & put them in a bowl. Then, pour lemon juice over the slices.

8. Put sheets of nori on a flat surface, wet your hands & spread ¾ to 1 cup of rice on each sheet. Press the rice into a thin layer, leaving ½-inch of nori on one long side.

9. To make California rolls, stack crabmeat, avocado, cucumber & carrot in a thin strip along the edge of 3 nori sheets opposite the edge that isn't covered.

10. For eggplant & avocado rolls, put a thin strip of eggplant & avocado on top of each other along the edge of 3 nori sheets opposite the edge left open.

11. To make pesto & egg rolls, spread pesto in a thin strip along with the edge opposite the open edge of 3 nori sheets & top with egg slices.

12. To make shrimp & asparagus rolls, put shrimp & asparagus on top of each other in a thin strip along the edge of 3 nori sheets opposite the open edge.

13. Move one prepared sheet of nori to a bamboo sushi mat. With the mat, roll the nori & rice around the filling until the edge of the nori that isn't covered shows. Wet the edge of the nori that sticks out & seal the roll. Each roll should be cut into 8 pieces. Do the same with the rest of the prepared nori.

Notes:

- There're of course many other types of sushi rolls. Look at a sushi restaurant's ingredients to get ideas for what to put inside the rolls. Also, try putting the fillings together in different ways. We tried different combinations & most of them seemed to work.
- Because one person didn't like nori, we took it out of a roll for her. If you do this, make sure you use enough rice & pack it tightly while rolling, or it will fall apart.
- Follow the directions for making California rolls, but use shrimp instead of crab meat. To make lobster rolls, follow the instructions for making California rolls, but use lobster instead of crab meat.
- Before rolling, you can sprinkle sesame seeds on the rice or add a small amount of wasabi. Substitute mango for avocado.
- If you want the rice to be on the outside of the roll, flip the nori over after you put the rice on it so that the rice side is down. Then fill & roll the nori.
- As the rolls are being made, the nori sheets can get softer. Before making the next roll, I always make the first one from start to finish.

Temari Sushi

Prep Time: 40 mins
Cook Time: 20 mins
Overall: 1 hr
Servings: 4
Calories (Per Serving): 350

Ingredients

- For Seasoned Lotus Root & Carrot

½-inch lotus root (renkon)
½-inch carrot
½ cup of dashi (Japanese soup stock)
1 tsp of sake
1 tsp of mirin
1 tsp of sugar
2 tsp usukuchi (light-colored) soy sauce (I use light color soy sauce, so the color doesn't become way too dark; you can use normal soy sauce)
⅛ tsp of kosher salt (Diamond Crystal; use half for table salt)

- Shredded Egg Crepe (Kinshi Tamago)

1 big egg (50 g w/o shell)
⅛ tsp kosher salt (Diamond Crystal; use ½ for table salt) (for egg)
1 tbsp neutral-flavored oil (vegetable, rice bran, canola, etc.)

- For Temari Sushi

5 rice cooker cups sushi rice (cooked & seasoned) (3 rice-cooker-cups (180-ml x 3 = 540-ml) yields around 5 ¼ US cups)
¼ avocado
¼ cup Sakura denbu (seasoned codfish flakes)
½ sheet nori (dried laver seaweed)
2 slices lemon
3 shiso leaves (perilla/ooba)
5 sprigs of chives

- For Sashimi Choices

sashimi-grade salmon
sashimi-grade tuna (maguro)
sashimi-grade sea bream (tai)
sashimi-grade yellowtail (Hamachi)
uni (sea urchin)
cooked shrimp
smoked salmon

Instructions

- To Make the Sushi Rice

1. Sushi rice, which is steamed rice seasoned with sweet vinegar, must be made first if you haven't already done so because it takes at least 1-hour & 40-min to prepare.

- To Make the Seasoned Lotus Root & Carrot

1. Put the lotus root, carrot & the rest of the ingredients in a small sauce-pan (seasoning). Bring it to a simmer & cook it until it's soft.

- To Make the Kinshi Tamago (Shredded Egg Crepe)

1. Whisk the egg & salt together in a bowl. On medium heat, heat oil in a pan that doesn't stick. Pour the beaten eggs into the pan & spread them out evenly. When the bottom side is done, flip it over. When the egg is done, take it out & cut it into thin strips with a chiffonade.

- To Make the Sushi Rice Balls

1. Put a piece of plastic wrap in top of the scale. Put

30g (2 tbsp) of sushi rice on the plastic wrap & roll it into a ball. Put the next batch on a plate & measure it. Make sure to put plastic wrap over the rice ball & a damp towel over the sushi rice to keep the rice from drying out.

- To Cut the Sashimi

    1. Slice the sashimi you want into thin pieces.

- To Make the Temari Sushi

    1. Put a sheet of plastic on the surface you'll be working on. Put the topping you want in the middle, such as sashimi, seasoned lotus, shredded egg crepe, etc. Then put the sushi rice ball on top of the ingredient. Twist the plastic wrap around the rice ball to make it tighter. Form it well so that it looks like a nice ball. Set aside.

    2. Keep going with the other ingredients you have already made.

    3. Add ikura, nori, greens, etc., to the top.

- For Storing:

    1. Fish that is good for sashimi has to be eaten within 24-hours. Put the leftovers in a container that won't let air in & put it in the fridge for a day. Temari sushi should be eaten as soon as possible, but it can be always kept in the fridge for up to 24-hours. I strongly suggest putting them inside an airtight container or a plate wrapped tightly in plastic. Then, wrap a thick kitchen towel around the container or plate, so the food stays safe in a cool place & the rice doesn't get hard from the cold air in the fridge.

Tempura Maki

Prep Time: 15 mins
Cook Time: 10 mins
Overall: 25 mins
Servings: 4 rolls
Calories (Per Serving): 350

Ingredients

4 nori sheets
1 cup mixed tempura vegetables
2 avocados, sliced
2 cups of prepared sushi rice
3 tbsp Japanese mayo
8 cooked shrimp

Instructions

1. In one pan, make the tempura batter. Then, add the vegetables & shrimp & fry them until they are light golden brown. Put paper towels down to dry.

2. Lay a nori sheet flat on a bamboo mat. Cover three quarters of the sheet with ½ cup of ready-made sushi rice.

3. Put two shrimp & fourteen vegetables in the middle of the rice. Spread some mayo on top & then add slices of avocado.

4. Lift the end of the mat that is at the bottom & roll it forward over the fillings.

5. Cut the roll into six to eight pieces. Do it again with rest of the ingredients.

6. Serve right away with pickled ginger, soy sauce & wasabi. Enjoy this maki that is crispy, creamy & tasty!

Tuna Tataki

Prep Time: 5 mins
Cook Time: 5 mins
Overall: 10 mins
Servings: 2
Calories (Per Serving): 255

Ingredients

½ lb. sashimi-grade yellowfin/ahi tuna
2 tbsp neutral-flavored oil (vegetable, rice bran, canola, etc.)
- Tataki Sauce:
1 green onion/scallion (1 tbsp chopped green onion)
1 knob ginger (1", 2.5 cm; 1 tsp grated)
3 tbsp ponzu
2 tsp roasted sesame oil
1 tsp soy sauce
1 tsp toasted white sesame seeds
- Garnish:
½ lemon
Korean chili thread

Instructions

1. Gather up all the ingredients together.
2. Grate the ginger & thinly slice the green onion.
3. Mix the ingredients for the tataki sauce in a small bowl.
4. Heat the oil in a pan that doesn't stick. Sear the tuna for 30-sec on each side when the oil is hot.
5. Once it is browned on all sides, take it off from the heat & let it cool. Cut the tuna into pieces that are ¼-inch (6 mm) long. Pour the sauce & dish it up.
- For Storing:
1. You can put the leftovers in a container that won't let air in & keep them in the fridge for a day.

Turkey Roll Sushi

Prep Time: 15 mins
Overall: 15 mins
Servings: 4
Yields: 4
Calories (Per Serving): 225

Ingredients

¾ cup fresh spinach, chopped

¼ cup cream cheese, softened

¼ cup of shredded Cheddar cheese, or more to taste

4 pickled peppers, chopped

½ spring onion (green part only), chopped, or more to taste

2 tsp garlic powder

¾ tsp ground black pepper

2 pinches red pepper flakes

2 flour tortillas

½ pound sliced deli turkey meat

Instructions

1. Mix together spinach, cream cheese, Cheddar cheese, pickled peppers, green onions, garlic powder, black pepper & red pepper flakes. Spread about 1-inch of the cream cheese mixture on the top of each tortilla. Save about 1 tbsp of the cream cheese mixture for sealing.

2. Place the turkey on top of the cream cheese mixture on each tortilla. Spread a thin line of the cream cheese mixture that was set aside under the turkey on each tortilla to keep it together. Starting with the end that has the most cream cheese mixture, roll up each tortilla around the filling & seal it with a very small amount of cream cheese mixture on the opposite end. Cut the roll into ½-inch-wide slices to make turkey "sushi" rolls.

- Notes

If you want, sprinkle more cheese on the row below the turkey before rolling it up.

To keep the rolls clean, wipe the knife after each cut.

Vegetarian Sushi

Prep Time: 45 mins
Cook Time: 15 mins
Extra Time: 10 mins
Overall: 1 hrs 10 mins
Servings: 4
Yields: 4 sushi rolls
Calories (Per Serving): 385

Ingredients

1 ½ cups uncooked short-grain white rice
1 ½ cups water
⅓ cup red wine vinegar
2 tsp white sugar
1 tsp salt
½ avocado - peeled, pitted & thinly sliced
1 tsp lemon juice
¼ cup sesame seeds, or as needed
½ cucumber - peeled, seeded & cut into matchsticks
½ green bell pepper, seeded & cut into matchsticks
½ zucchini, cut into matchsticks

Instructions

1. Put the rice & water in a sauce-pan over high heat. Bring it to boil & then turn down the heat slowly to very low. Cover with a tight-fitting lid & cook on low heat for about 15-min, or until all the water is absorbed. Take the rice off the heat & let it sit for 10-min with the lid on.

2. Mix together red wine vinegar, sugar & salt until the sugar is gone. Move the rice to a large bowl & fluff it with a fork. Pour the vinegar mixture over the rice & stir to coat it. Spread the rice out on a large piece of parchment paper & fan it until it is cool. Wet paper towels are used to cover the rice.

3. In a bowl, sprinkle avocado slices with lemon juice.

4. Spread some sesame seeds in a thin layer on a sushi mat. Take about half a cup of the cooled rice & spread out in an even layer on the sushi mat. Line up ¼ of the slices of cucumber, avocado, bell pepper & zucchini in the middle of the rice.

5. Pick up the edge of the sushi mat, then fold the bottom edge of the sheet up to cover the filling & roll the sushi tightly into a thick cylinder. Once the sushi is rolled, place it on the mat & squeeze it gently to make it tight. Use the rest of the ingredients the same way to make 4 rolls. Put the rolls on a serving plate, cut each roll into 6 or 8 pieces & cover with wet paper towels until it's time to serve.

Vegetarian Sushi Platter

Prep Time: 35 mins
Cook Time: 10 mins
Overall: 45 mins
Servings: 32 pieces
Calories (Per Serving): 250

Ingredients

1 cup julienned cucumbers
1 cup of julienned carrots
1 ripe avocado, sliced
12 asparagus stalks, blanched
2 cups sushi rice
6 nori sheets
Wasabi paste & pickled ginger

Instructions

1. Evenly spread ½ cup of cooked sushi rice over ¾ of the nori sheet.

2. Put vegetables like cucumbers, avocado, asparagus, carrots & so on across the middle of the rice.

3. Use a bamboo rolling mat to gently roll up the sushi roll away from you.

4. Take the mat off & use a clean sharp knife to cut the roll into four pieces.

5. Use the rest of the ingredients to make a few creative veggie sushi rolls.

6. Put together a colorful platter of veggie sushi & serve right away with wasabi & pickled ginger. Enjoy!

Watermelon-Cucumber Salad with Vinegar & Lime

Prep Time: 20 mins
Overall: 20 mins
Servings: 10
Yields: 10
Calories (Per Serving): 65

Ingredients

2 cucumbers
4 cups cubed seeded watermelon
½ cup finely chopped red onion
3 tbsp seasoned rice vinegar
3 tbsp white wine vinegar
3 tbsp lime juice
¼ cup chopped fresh mint
½ cup feta cheese

Instructions

    1. Use a vegetable peeler to make stripes on the length of a cucumber. Cut cucumbers in half along their length & then cut each half into ¼-inch slices to make "half-moon" shapes. Mix cucumbers, watermelon & red onion.

    2. Mix rice vinegar, white wine vinegar, lime juice & mint. Mix the mint by vigorously stirring & pressing the leaves with a spoon until they look bruised but aren't falling apart. Take off & throw away mint leaves.

    3. Pour the dressing over the salad & then toss it gently. Sprinkle feta cheese over the salad; toss gently.

Yellowtail Roll

Prep Time: 30 mins
Overall: 30 mins
Servings: 2
Calories (Per Serving): 180

Ingredients

1 ½ cup sushi rice (cooked & seasoned)
3.3 oz sashimi-grade yellowtail
1 sheet nori (dried laver seaweed) (cut in half crosswise)
3 tbsp green onions/scallions (chopped)
- For Tezu (vinegared finger-dipping water):

¼ cup water
2 tsp rice vinegar (unseasoned)
- For Serving:

soy sauce
wasabi
pickled red ginger (Beni shoga or kizami Beni shoga)

Instructions

1. Gather up all the ingredients together.

2. Yellowtail should be cut into cubes that are ¼-inch (6 mm) & chopped into smaller pieces.

3. Place a sheet of nori with the shiny side on the down on the bamboo mat that is covered in plastic. Wet your fingers with Tezu & spread ¾ cup of rice evenly on the nori sheet.

4. Put half of the chopped yellowtail at the end of the nori sheet that is closest to the bottom.

5. Line the bottom edge of the bamboo mat with a nori sheet. Hold the fillings in place with your fingers, grab the bottom edge of the bamboo mat & roll it into a tight cylinder. Pick up the edge of the bamboo mat & roll it forward while keeping a light touch on it.

6. Cut the roll in half with a very sharp knife & then cut each half into 3–4 pieces. Every few cuts, wipe the knife with a damp cloth. Serve the sushi with wasabi, soy sauce & pickled ginger.

- For Storing:

1. Sushi rolls are best when eaten the same day they are made. Rice gets dry & hard when it's in the fridge. So, if you really want to keep sushi rolls in the fridge, I suggest covering them with plastic wrap & then a thick kitchen towel. This will keep the rice safe & cool, but not cold.

If you're reading this,
You're Amazing!

Thank you so much for choosing our cookbook as your culinary companion! We appreciate your support & hope that you find our collection of recipes inspiring & enjoyable. As promised, this last page serves as a platform for additional information & personal thoughts. Firstly, we would like to address the absence of images throughout the cookbook. We decided to exclude images due to the significant increase in production costs that would have resulted. Our main priority is to provide you with a comprehensive selection of restaurant kitchen tested & top recommended recipes while keeping the book affordable. We believe that the quality & reliability of our recipes will guide you through the cooking process seamlessly, even without accompanying visuals. We are confident in the authenticity & deliciousness of the recipes. Each recipe has undergone thorough testing, ensuring that they meet our high standards in terms of taste, texture, & overall satisfaction. We have carefully selected these recipes to offer you a diverse range of flavors & culinary experiences. Join us on this adventurous cooking journey, & together with Team Lei Yanmei, let's explore the delightful world of flavors, aromas, & creativity. We value your participation & look forward to hearing about your culinary triumphs & discoveries.

If you are satisfied with our effort, we would greatly appreciate it if you could take just 5 seconds to leave a review. Your feedback means the world to us & helps small businesses like ours to thrive. Your simple act of sharing your thoughts will motivate & support our culinary endeavors. Thank you once again for joining us on this tasty adventure!

To give your valuable feedback on Amazon, scan:

Mail me at lei.yanmei@chef.net

Check out more deals like this at amazon.com/Lei-Yanmei/e/B0BK7DHMZK

Made in United States
Troutdale, OR
12/01/2023

15184101R00044